MW00947699

Amazon Web Services Tutorial

The Ultimate Beginner's Guide

© 2017 COPYRIGHT

DISCLAIMERS

We are not lawyers. This website and the content provided herein are simply for educational purposes and do not take the place of legal advice from your attorney. Every effort has been made to ensure that the content provided on this website is accurate and helpful for our readers at publishing time. However, this is not an exhaustive treatment of the subjects. No liability is assumed for losses or damages due to the information provided. You are responsible for your own choices, actions, and results. You should consult your attorney for your specific publishing and disclaimer questions and needs.

This is a work of fiction. Names, characters, places, and incidents either are the products of the author's imagination or are used fictitiously. Any resemblance to actual persons, living or dead, businesses, companies, events, or locales is entirely coincidental.

Amazon Web Services Tutorial

Amazon Web Services (AWS) is Amazon's cloud web hosting platform that offers flexible, reliable, scalable, easy-to-use, and cost-effective solutions. This tutorial covers various important topics illustrating how AWS works and how it is beneficial to run your website on Amazon Web Services.

Audience

This tutorial is prepared for beginners who want to learn how Amazon Web Services works to provide reliable, flexible, and cost-effective cloud computing services.

Prerequisites

To benefit from this tutorial, you should have the desire to understand how Amazon Web Services can help you scale your cloud computing services.

Table of Contents

Amazon Web Services - Cloud Computing

In 2006, **Amazon Web Services (AWS)** started to offer IT services to the market in the form of web servicles, which is nowadays known as **cloud computing**. With this cloud, we need not plan for servers and other IT infrastructure which takes up much of time in advance. Instead, these services can instantly spin up hundreds or thousands of servers in minutes and deliver results faster. We pay only for what we use with no up-front expenses and no long-term commitments, which makes AWS cost efficient.

Today, AWS provides a highly reliable, scalable, low-cost infrastructure platform in the cloud that powers multitude of businesses in 190 countries around the world.

What is Cloud Computing?

Cloud computing is an internet-based computing service in which large groups of remote servers are networked to allow centralized data storage, and online access to computer services or resources.

Using cloud computing, organizations can use shared computing and storage resources rather than building, operating, and improving infrastructure on their own.

Cloud computing is a model that enables the following features.

- Users can provision and release resources on-demand.
- Resources can be scaled up or down automatically, depending on the load.
- Resources are accessible over a network with proper security.
- Cloud service providers can enable a pay-as-you-go model, where customers are charged based on the type of resources and per usage.

Types of Clouds

There are three types of clouds — Public, Private, and Hybrid cloud.

Public Cloud

In public cloud, the third-party service providers make resources and services available to their customers via Internet. Customer's data and related security is with the service providers' owned infrastructure.

Private Cloud

A private cloud also provides almost similar features as public cloud, but the data and services are managed by the organization or by the third party only for the customer's organization. In this type of cloud, major control is over the infrastructure so security related issues are minimized.

Hybrid Cloud

A hybrid cloud is the combination of both private and public cloud. The decision to run on private or public cloud usually depends on various parameters like sensitivity of data and applications, industry certifications and required standards, regulations, etc.

Cloud Service Models

There are three types of service models in cloud – IaaS, PaaS, and SaaS.

IaaS

IaaS stands for **Infrastructure as a Service**. It provides users with the capability to provision processing, storage, and network connectivity on demand. Using this service model, the customers can develop their own applications on these resources.

PaaS

PaaS stands for **Platform as a Service**. Here, the service provider provides various services like databases, queues, workflow engines, e-mails, etc. to their customers. The customer can then use these components for building their own applications. The services, availability of resources and data backup are handled by the service provider that helps the customers to focus more on their application's functionality.

SaaS

SaaS stands for **Software as a Service**. As the name suggests, here the third-party providers provide end-user applications to their customers with some administrative capability at the application level, such as the ability to create and manage their users. Also some level of customizability is possible such as the customers can use their own corporate logos, colors, etc.

Advantages of Cloud Computing

Here is a list of some of the most important advantages that Cloud Computing has to offer —

- **Cost-Efficient** — Building our own servers and tools is time-consuming as well as expensive as we need to order, pay for, install, and configure expensive hardware, long before we need it. However, using cloud computing, we only pay for the amount we use and when we use the computing resources. In this manner, cloud computing is cost efficient.
- **Reliability** — A cloud computing platform provides much more managed, reliable and consistent service than an in-house IT infrastructure. It guarantees 24x7 and 365 days of service. If any of the server fails, then hosted applications and services can easily be transited to any of the available servers.
- **Unlimited Storage** — Cloud computing provides almost unlimited storage capacity, i.e., we need not worry about running out of storage space or increasing our current storage space availability. We can access as much or as little as we need.
- **Backup & Recovery** — Storing data in the cloud, backing it up and restoring the same is relatively easier than storing it on a physical device. The cloud service providers also have enough technology to recover our data, so there is the convenience of recovering our data anytime.
- **Easy Access to Information** — Once you register yourself in cloud, you can access your account from anywhere in the world provided there is internet connection at that point. There are various storage and security facilities that vary with the account type chosen.

Disadvantages of Cloud Computing

Although Cloud Computing provides a wonderful set of advantages, it has some drawbacks as well that often raise questions about its efficiency.

Security issues

Security is the major issue in cloud computing. The cloud service providers implement the best security standards and industry certifications, however, storing data and important files on external service providers always bears a risk.

AWS cloud infrastructure is designed to be the most flexible and secured cloud network. It provides scalable and highly reliable platform that enables customers to deploy applications and data quickly and securely.

Technical issues

As cloud service providers offer services to number of clients each day, sometimes the system can have some serious issues leading to business processes temporarily being suspended. Additionally, if the internet connection is offline then we will not be able to access any of the applications, server, or data from the cloud.

Not easy to switch service providers

Cloud service providers promises vendors that the cloud will be flexible to use and integrate, however switching cloud services is not easy. Most organizations may find it difficult to host and integrate current cloud applications on another platform. Interoperability and support issues may arise such as applications developed on Linux platform may not work properly on Microsoft Development Framework (.Net).

Amazon Web Services - Basic Architecture

This is the basic structure of **AWS EC2**, where **EC2** stands for Elastic Compute Cloud. EC2 allow users to use virtual machines of different configurations as per their requirement. It allows various configuration options, mapping of individual server, various pricing options, etc. We will discuss these in detail in AWS Products section. Following is the diagrammatic representation of the architecture.

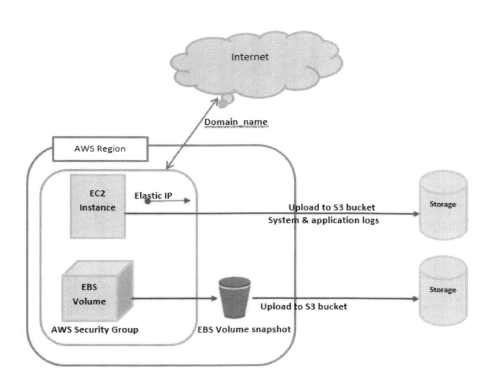

Note – In the above diagram **S3** stands for Simple Storage Service. It allows the users to store and retrieve various types of data using API calls. It doesn't contain any computing element. We will discuss this topic in detail in AWS products section.

Load Balancing

Load balancing simply means to hardware or software load over web servers, that improver's the efficiency of the server as well as the application. Following is the diagrammatic representation of AWS architecture with load balancing.

Hardware load balancer is a very common network appliance used in traditional web application architectures.

AWS provides the Elastic Load Balancing service, it distributes the traffic to EC2 instances across multiple available sources, and dynamic addition and removal of Amazon EC2 hosts from the load-balancing rotation.

Elastic Load Balancing can dynamically grow and shrink the load-balancing capacity to adjust to traffic demands and also support sticky sessions to address more advanced routing needs.

Amazon Cloud-front

It is responsible for content delivery, i.e. used to deliver website. It may contain dynamic, static, and streaming content using a global network of edge locations. Requests for content at the user's end are automatically routed to the nearest edge location, which improves the performance.

Amazon Cloud-front is optimized to work with other Amazon Web Services, like Amazon S3 and Amazon EC2. It also works fine with any non-AWS origin server and stores the original files in a similar manner.

In Amazon Web Services, there are no contracts or monthly commitments. We pay only for as much or as little content as we deliver through the service.

Elastic Load Balancer

It is used to spread the traffic to web servers, which improves performance. AWS provides the Elastic Load Balancing service, in which traffic is distributed to EC2 instances over multiple available zones, and dynamic addition and removal of Amazon EC2 hosts from the load-balancing rotation.

Elastic Load Balancing can dynamically grow and shrink the load-balancing capacity as per the traffic conditions.

Security Management

Amazon's Elastic Compute Cloud (EC2) provides a feature called security groups, which is similar to an inbound network firewall, in which we have to specify the protocols, ports, and source IP ranges that are allowed to reach your EC2 instances.

Each EC2 instance can be assigned one or more security groups, each of which routes the appropriate traffic to each instance. Security groups can be configured using specific subnets or IP addresses which limits access to EC2 instances.

Elastic Caches

Amazon Elastic Cache is a web service that manages the memory cache in the cloud. In memory management, cache has a very important role and helps to reduce the load on the services, improves the performance and scalability on the database tier by caching frequently used information.

Amazon RDS

Amazon RDS (Relational Database Service) provides a similar access as that of MySQL, Oracle, or Microsoft SQL Server database engine. The same queries, applications, and tools can be used with Amazon RDS.

It automatically patches the database software and manages backups as per the user's instruction. It also supports point-in-time recovery. There are no up-front investments required, and we pay only for the resources we use.

Hosting RDMS on EC2 Instances

Amazon RDS allows users to install RDBMS (Relational Database Management System) of your choice like MySQL, Oracle, SQL Server, DB2, etc. on an EC2 instance and can manage as required.

Amazon EC2 uses Amazon EBS (Elastic Block Storage) similar to network-attached storage. All data and logs running on EC2 instances should be placed on Amazon EBS volumes, which will be available even if the database host fails.

Amazon EBS volumes automatically provide redundancy within the availability zone, which increases the availability of simple disks. Further if the volume is not sufficient for our databases needs, volume can be added to increase the performance for our database.

Using Amazon RDS, the service provider manages the storage and we only focus on managing the data.

Storage & Backups

AWS cloud provides various options for storing, accessing, and backing up web application data and assets. The Amazon S3 (Simple Storage Service) provides a simple web-services interface that can be used to store and retrieve any amount of data, at any time, from anywhere on the web.

Amazon S3 stores data as objects within resources called **buckets**. The user can store as many objects as per requirement within the bucket, and can read, write and delete objects from the bucket.

Amazon EBS is effective for data that needs to be accessed as block storage and requires persistence beyond the life of the running instance, such as database partitions and application logs.

Amazon EBS volumes can be maximized up to 1 TB, and these volumes can be striped for larger volumes and increased performance. Provisioned IOPS volumes are designed to meet the needs of database workloads that are sensitive to storage performance and consistency.

Amazon EBS currently supports up to 1,000 IOPS per volume. We can stripe multiple volumes together to deliver thousands of IOPS per instance to an application.

Auto Scaling

The difference between AWS cloud architecture and the traditional hosting model is that AWS can dynamically scale the web application fleet on demand to handle changes in traffic.

In the traditional hosting model, traffic forecasting models are generally used to provision hosts ahead of projected traffic. In AWS, instances can be provisioned on the fly according to a set of triggers for scaling the fleet out and back in. Amazon Auto Scaling can create capacity groups of servers that can grow or shrink on demand.

Key Considerations for Web Hosting in AWS

Following are some of the key considerations for web hosting —

No physical network devices needed

In AWS, network devices like firewalls, routers, and load-balancers for AWS applications no longer reside on physical devices and are replaced with software solutions.

Multiple options are available to ensure quality software solutions. For load balancing choose Zeus, HAProxy, Nginx, Pound, etc. For establishing a VPN connection choose OpenVPN, OpenSwan, Vyatta, etc.

No security concerns

AWS provides a more secured model, in which every host is locked down. In Amazon EC2, security groups are designed for each type of host in the architecture, and a large variety of simple and tiered security models can be created to enable minimum access among hosts within your architecture as per requirement.

Availability of data centers

EC2 instances are easily available at most of the availability zones in AWS region and provides model for deploying your application across data centers for both high availability and reliability.

AWS - Management Console

AWS Management Console is a web application for managing Amazon Web Services. AWS Management Console consists of list of various services to choose from. It also provides all information related to our account like billing.

This console provides an inbuilt user interface to perform AWS tasks like working with Amazon S3 buckets, launching and connecting to Amazon EC2 instances, setting Amazon CloudWatch alarms, etc.

Following is the screenshot of AWS management console for Amazon EC2 service.

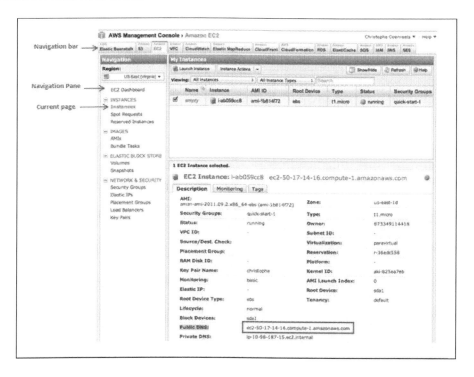

How to Access AWS?

Step 1 – Click on services. We get a list of various services.

Step 2 – Select the choice from the list of categories and we get their sub-categories such as Computer and Database category is selected in the following screenshots.

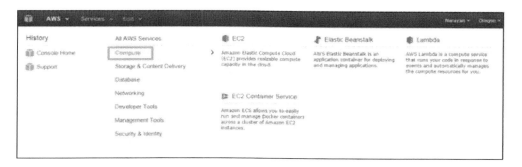

Step 3 – Select the service of your choice and the console of that service will open.

Customizing the Dashboard

Creating Services Shortcuts

Click the Edit menu on the navigation bar and a list of services appears. We can create their shortcuts by simply dragging them from the menu bar to the navigation bar.

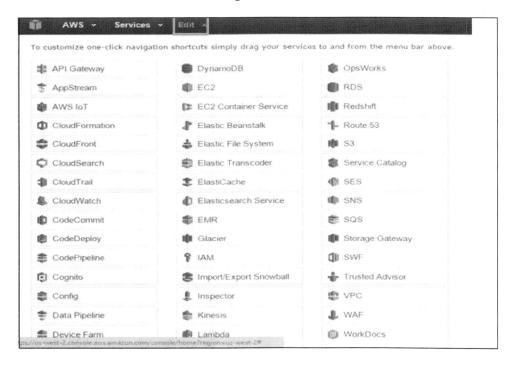

Adding Services Shortcuts

When we drag the service from the menu bar to the navigation bar, the shortcut will be created and added. We can also arrange them in any order. In the following screenshot we have created shortcut for S3, EMR and DynamoDB services.

Deleting Services Shortcuts

To delete the shortcut, click the edit menu and drag the shortcut from the navigation bar to the service menu. The shortcut will be removed. In the following screenshot, we have removed the shortcut for EMR services.

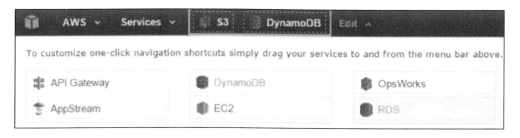

Selecting a Region

Many of the services are region specific and we need to select a region so that resources can be managed. Some of the services do not require a region to be selected like AWS Identity and Access Management (IAM).

To select a region, first we need to select a service. Click the Oregon menu (on the left side of the console) and then select a region

Changing the Password

We can change password of our AWS account. To change the password, following are the steps.

Step 1 – Click the account name on the left side of the navigation bar.

Step 2 – Choose Security Credentials and a new page will open having various options. Select the password option to change the password and follow the instructions.

Step 3 – After signing-in, a page opens again having certain options to change the password and follow the instructions.

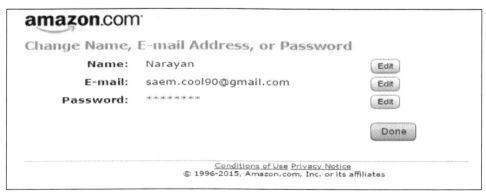

When successful, we will receive a confirmation message.

Know Your Billing Information

Click the account name in the navigation bar and select the 'Billing & Cost Management' option.

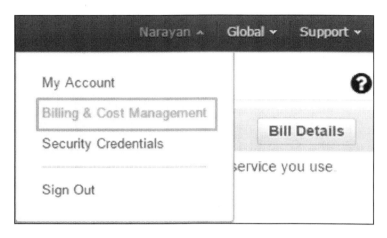

Now a new page will open having all the information related to money section. Using this service, we can pay AWS bills, monitor our usage and budget estimation.

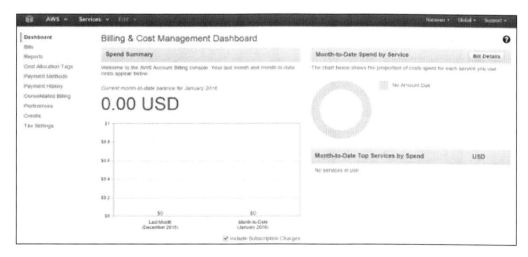

Amazon Web Services - Console Mobile App

The AWS Console mobile app, provided by Amazon Web Services, allows its users to view resources for select services and also supports a limited set of management functions for select resource types.

Following are the various services and supported functions that can be accessed using the mobile app.

EC2 (Elastic Compute Cloud)

- Browse, filter and search instances.
- View configuration details.
- Check status of CloudWatch metrics and alarms.
- Perform operations over instances like start, stop, reboot, termination.
- Manage security group rules.
- Manage Elastic IP Addresses.
- View block devices.

Elastic Load Balancing

- Browse, filter and search load balancers.
- View configuration details of attached instances.
- Add and remove instances from load balancers.

S3

- Browse buckets and view their properties.
- View properties of objects.

Route 53

- Browse and view hosted zones.
- Browse and view details of record sets.

RDS (Relational Database Service)

- Browse, filter, search and reboot instances.
- View configuration details, security and network settings.

Auto Scaling

- View group details, policies, metrics and alarms.
- Manage the number of instances as per the situation.

Elastic Beanstalk

- View applications and events.
- View environment configuration and swap environment CNAMEs.
- Restart app servers.

DynamoDB

- View tables and their details like metrics, index, alarms, etc.

CloudFormation

- View stack status, tags, parameters, output, events, and resources.

OpsWorks

- View configuration details of stack, layers, instances and applications.
- View instances, its logs, and reboot them.

CloudWatch

- View CloudWatch graphs of resources.
- List CloudWatch alarms by status and time.
- Action configurations for alarms.

Services Dashboard

- Provides information of available services and their status.
- All information related to the billing of the user.
- Switch the users to see the resources in multiple accounts.

Features of AWS Mobile App

To have access to the AWS Mobile App, we must have an existing AWS account. Simply create an identity using the account credentials and select the region in the menu. This app allows us to stay signed in to multiple identities at the same time.

For security reasons, it is recommended to secure the device with a passcode and to use an IAM user's credentials to log in to the app. In case the device is lost, then the IAM user can be deactivated to prevent unauthorized access.

Root accounts cannot be deactivated via mobile console. While using AWS Multi-Factor Authentication (MFA), it is recommended to use either a hardware MFA device or a virtual MFA on a separate mobile device for account security reasons.

The latest version is 1.14. There is a feedback link in the App's menu to share our experiences and for any queries.

Amazon Web Services - Account

How to Use AWS Account?

Following are the steps to access AWS services —

- Create an AWS account.
- Sign-up for AWS services.
- Create your password and access your account credentials.
- Activate your services in credits section.

Create an AWS Account

Amazon provides a fully functional free account for one year for users to use and learn the different components of AWS. You get access to AWS services like EC2, S3, DynamoDB, etc. for free. However, there are certain limitations based on the resources consumed.

Step 1 — To create an AWS account, open this link https://aws.amazon.com and sign-up for new account and enter the required details.

If we already have an account, then we can sign-in using the existing AWS password.

Step 2 – After providing an email-address, complete this form. Amazon uses this information for billing, invoicing and identifying the account. After creating the account, sign-up for the services needed.

▼Contact Information

Full Name:*

Address:*

City:*

State:

Postal Code:*

Country:* IN

Phone Number:*

Company Name:

Website URL:

* Denotes required field

Step 3 – To sign-up for the services, enter the payment information. Amazon executes a minimal amount transaction against the card on the file to check that it is valid. This charge varies with the region.

Step 4 – Next, is the identity verification. Amazon does a call back to verify the provided contact number.

Step 5 – Choose a support plan. Subscribe to one of the plans like Basic, Developer, Business, or Enterprise. The basic plan costs nothing and has limited resources, which is good to get familiar with AWS.

Step 6 – The final step is confirmation. Click the link to login again and it redirects to AWS management console.

Now the account is created and can be used to avail AWS services.

AWS Account Identifiers

AWS assigns two unique IDs to each AWS account.

- An AWS account ID
- A conical user ID

AWS Account ID

It is a 12-digit number like 123456789000 and is used to construct Amazon Resource Names (ARN). This ID helps to distinguish our resources from resources in other AWS accounts.

To know the AWS account number, click Support on the upper right side of the navigation bar in AWS management console as shown in the following screenshot.

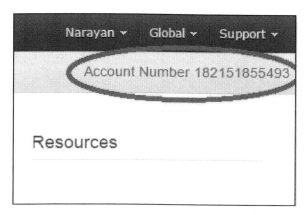

Conical String User ID

It is a long string of alphanumeric characters like 1234abcdef1234. This ID is used in Amazon S3 bucket policy for cross-account access, i.e. to access resources in another AWS account.

Account Alias

Account alias is the URL for your sign-in page and contains the account ID by default. We can customize this URL with the company name and even overwrite the previous one.

How to Create/Delete Your Own AWS Account Alias?

Step 1 – Sign in to the AWS management console and open the IAM console using the following link https://console.aws.amazon.com/iam/

Step 2 – Select the customize link and create an alias of choice.

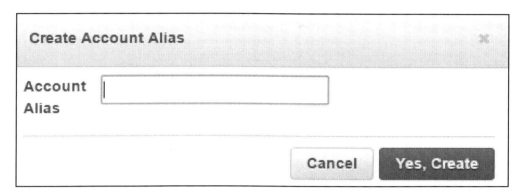

Step 3 – To delete the alias, click the customize link, then click the Yes, Delete button. This deletes the alias and it reverts to the Account ID.

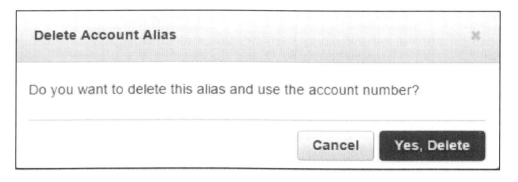

Multi Factor Authentication

Multi Factor Authentication (MFA) provides additional security by authenticating the users to enter a unique authentication code from an approved authentication device or SMS text message when they access AWS websites or services. If the MFA code is correct, then only the user can access AWS services or else not.

Requirements

To use MFA services, the user has to assign a device (hardware or virtual) to IAM user or AWS root account. Each MFA device assigned to the user must be unique, i.e. the user cannot enter a code from another user's device to authenticate.

How to Enable MFA Device?

Step 1 – Open the following link, https://console.aws.amazon.com/iam/

Step 2 – On the web page, choose users from the navigation pane on the right side to view the list of user name.

Step 3 – Scroll down to security credentials and choose MFA. Click activate MFA.

Step 4 – Follow the instructions and the MFA device will get activated with the account.

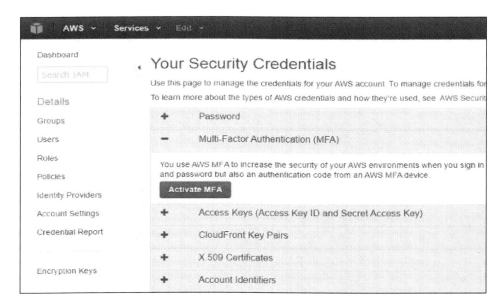

There are 3 ways to enable a MFA device —

SMS MFA Device

In this method, MFA requires us to configure the IAM user with the phone number of the user's SMS-compatible mobile device. When the user signs in, AWS sends a six-digit code by SMS text message to the user's mobile device. The user is required to enter the same code on a second web page during sign-in to authenticate the right user. This SMS-based MFA cannot be used with AWS root account.

Hardware MFA Device

In this method, MFA requires us to assign an MFA device (hardware) to the IAM user or the AWS root account. The device generates a six-digit numeric code based upon a time synchronized one-time password algorithm. The user has to enter the same code from the device on a second web page during sign-in to authenticate the right user.

Virtual MFA Device

In this method, MFA requires us to assign an MFA device (virtual) to the IAM user or the AWS root account. A virtual device is a software application (mobile app) running on a mobile device that emulates a physical device. The device generates a six-digit numeric code based upon a time-synchronized one-time password algorithm. The user has to enter the same code from the device on a second web page during sign-in to authenticate the right user.

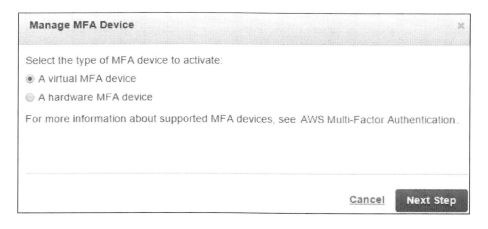

AWS Identity & Access Management (IAM)

IAM is a user entity which we create in AWS to represent a person that uses it with limited access to resources. Hence, we do not have to use the root account in our day-to-day activities as the root account has unrestricted access to our AWS resources.

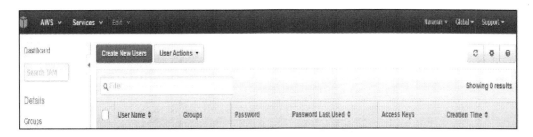

How to Create Users in IAM?

Step 1 – Open the link https://console.aws.amazon.com/iam/ to sign-in to AWS Management console.

Step 2 – Select the Users option on the left navigation pane to open the list of all users.

Step 3 – We can also create New Users using the Create New Users option, a new window will open. Enter the user-name which we want to create. Select the create option and a new user will be created.

Step 4 – We can also see Access Key IDs and secret keys by selecting Show Users Security Credentials link. We can also save these details on the computer using the Download Credentials option.

Step 5 – We can manage the user's own security credentials like creating password, managing MFA devices, managing security certificates, creating/deleting access keys, adding user to groups, etc.

There are many more features that are optional and are available on the web page.

AWS - Elastic Compute Cloud

Amazon EC2 (Elastic Compute Cloud) is a web service interface that provides resizable compute capacity in the AWS cloud. It is designed for developers to have complete control over web-scaling and computing resources.

EC2 instances can be resized and the number of instances scaled up or down as per our requirement. These instances can be launched in one or more geographical locations or regions, and **Availability Zones (AZs)**. Each region comprises of several AZs at distinct locations, connected by low latency networks in the same region.

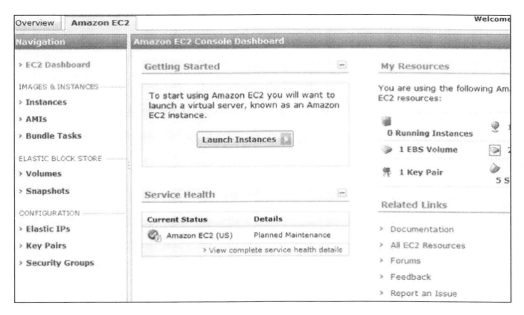

EC2 Components

In AWS EC2, the users must be aware about the EC2 components, their operating systems support, security measures, pricing structures, etc.

Operating System Support

Amazon EC2 supports multiple OS in which we need to pay additional licensing fees like: Red Hat Enterprise, SUSE Enterprise and Oracle Enterprise Linux, UNIX, Windows Server, etc. These OS needs to be implemented in conjunction with Amazon Virtual Private Cloud (VPC).

Security

Users have complete control over the visibility of their AWS account. In AWS EC2, the security systems allow create groups and place running instances into it as per the requirement. You can specify the groups with which other groups may communicate, as well as the groups with which IP subnets on the Internet may talk.

Pricing

AWS offers a variety of pricing options, depending on the type of resources, types of applications and database. It allows the users to configure their resources and compute the charges accordingly.

Fault tolerance

Amazon EC2 allows the users to access its resources to design fault-tolerant applications. EC2 also comprises geographic regions and isolated locations known as availability zones for fault tolerance and stability. It doesn't share the exact locations of regional data centers for security reasons.

When the users launch an instance, they must select an AMI that's in the same region where the instance will run. Instances are distributed across multiple availability zones to provide continuous services in failures, and Elastic IP (EIPs) addresses are used to quickly map failed instance addresses to concurrent running instances in other zones to avoid delay in services.

Migration

This service allows the users to move existing applications into EC2. It costs $80.00 per storage device and $2.49 per hour for data loading. This service suits those users having large amount of data to move.

Features of EC2

Here is a list of some of the prominent features of EC2 —

- **Reliable** — Amazon EC2 offers a highly reliable environment where replacement of instances is rapidly possible. Service Level Agreement commitment is 99.9% availability for each Amazon EC2 region.
- **Designed for Amazon Web Services** — Amazon EC2 works fine with Amazon services like Amazon S3, Amazon RDS, Amazon DynamoDB, and Amazon SQS. It provides a complete solution for computing, query processing, and storage across a wide range of applications.
- **Secure** — Amazon EC2 works in Amazon Virtual Private Cloud to provide a secure and robust network to resources.
- **Flexible Tools** — Amazon EC2 provides the tools for developers and system administrators to build failure applications and isolate themselves from common failure situations.
- **Inexpensive** — Amazon EC2 wants us to pay only for the resources that we use. It includes multiple purchase plans such as On-Demand Instances, Reserved Instances, Spot Instances, etc. which we can choose as per our requirement.

How to Use AWS EC2

Step 1 – Sign-in to AWS account and open IAM console by using the following link https://console.aws.amazon.com/iam/.

Step 2 – In the navigation Panel, create/view groups and follow the instructions.

Step 3 – Create IAM user. Choose users in the navigation pane. Then create new users and add users to the groups.

Step 4 – Create a Virtual Private Cloud using the following instructions.

- Open the Amazon VPC console by using the following link – https://console.aws.amazon.com/vpc/
- Select VPC from the navigation panel. Then select the same region in which we have created key-pair.
- Select start VPC wizard on VPC dashboard.
- Select VPC configuration page and make sure that VPC with single subnet is selected. The choose Select.
- VPC with a single public subnet page will open. Enter the VPC name in the name field and leave other configurations as default.
- Select create VPC, then select Ok.

Step 5 – Create WebServerSG security groups and add rules using the following instructions.

- On the VPC console, select Security groups in the navigation panel.
- Select create security group and fill the required details like group name, name tag, etc.
- Select your VPC ID from the menu. Then select yes, create button.

- Now a group is created. Select the edit option in the inbound rules tab to create rules.

Step 6 – Launch EC2 instance into VPC using the following instructions.

- Open EC2 console by using the following link – https://console.aws.amazon.com/ec2/
- Select launch instance option in the dashboard.
- A new page will open. Choose Instance Type and provide the configuration. Then select Next: Configure Instance Details.
- A new page will open. Select VPC from the network list. Select subnet from the subnet list and leave the other settings as default.
- Click Next until the Tag Instances page appears.

Step 7 – On the Tag Instances page, provide a tag with a name to the instances. Select Next: Configure Security Group.

Step 8 – On the Configure Security Group page, choose the Select an existing security group option. Select the WebServerSG group that we created previously, and then choose Review and Launch.

Step 9 – Check Instance details on Review Instance Launch page then click the Launch button.

Step 10 – A pop up dialog box will open. Select an existing key pair or create a new key pair. Then select the acknowledgement check box and click the Launch Instances button.

Amazon Web Services - Auto Scaling

As the name suggests, auto scaling allows you to scale your Amazon EC2 instances up or down automatically as per the instructions set by the user. Parameters like minimum and maximum number of instances are set by the user. Using this, the number of Amazon EC2 instances you're using increases automatically as the demand rises to maintain the performance, and decreases automatically as the demand decreases to minimize the cost.

Auto Scaling is particularly effective for those applications that fluctuate on hourly, daily, or weekly usage. Auto Scaling is enabled by Amazon CloudWatch and is available at no extra cost. AWS CloudWatch can be used to measure CPU utilization, network traffic, etc.

Elastic Load Balancing

Elastic Load Balancing (ELB) automatically distributes incoming request traffic across multiple Amazon EC2 instances and results in achieving higher fault tolerance. It detects unfit instances and automatically reroutes traffic to fit instances until the unfit instances have been restored in a round-robin manner. However, if we need more complex routing algorithms, then choose other services like Amazon Route53.

ELB consists of the following three components.

Load Balancer

This includes monitoring and handling the requests incoming through the Internet/intranet and distributes them to EC2 instances registered with it.

Control Service

This includes automatically scaling of handling capacity in response to incoming traffic by adding and removing load balancers as required. It also performs fitness check of instances.

SSL Termination

ELB provides SSL termination that saves precious CPU cycles, encoding and decoding SSL within your EC2 instances attached to the ELB. An X.509 certificate is required to be configured within the ELB. This SSL connection in the EC2 instance is optional, we can also terminate it.

Features of ELB

Following are the most prominent features of ELB —

- ELS is designed to handle unlimited requests per second with gradually increasing load pattern.
- We can configure EC2 instances and load balancers to accept traffic.
- We can add/remove load balancers as per requirement without affecting the overall flow of information.
- It is not designed to handle sudden increase in requests like online exams, online trading, etc.

• Customers can enable Elastic Load Balancing within a single Availability Zone or across multiple zones for even more consistent application performance.

How to Create Load Balancers?

Step 1 – Go to Amazon EC2 console using this link – https://console.aws.amazon.com/ec2/.

Step 2 – Select your load balancer region from the region menu on the right side.

Step 3 – Select Load Balancers from the navigation pane and choose Create Load Balancer option. A pop-up window will open and we need to provide the required details.

Step 4 – In load Balancer name box: Enter name of your load balancer.

Step 5 – In create LB inside box: Select the same network which you have selected for instances.

Step 6 – Select Enable advanced VPC configuration, if selected default VPC.

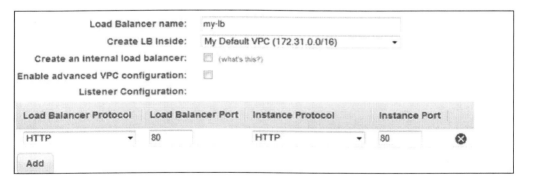

Step 7 – Click the Add button and a new pop-up will appear to select subnets from the list of available subnets as shown in the following screenshot. Select only one subnet per availability zone.

This window will not appear if we do not select Enable advanced VPC configuration.

Available Subnets				
Actions	Availability Zone	Subnet ID	Subnet CIDR	Name
⊕	us-west-2c	subnet-cb663da2	10.0.1.0/24	
⊕	us-west-2c	subnet-c9663da0	10.0.0.0/24	
Selected Subnets				
Actions	Availability Zone	Subnet ID	Subnet CIDR	Name
⊖	us-west-2a	subnet-e4f33493	10.0.2.0/24	
⊖	us-west-2b	subnet-5264e837	10.0.3.0/24	

Step 8 – Choose Next; a pop-up window will open. After selecting a VPC as your network, assign security groups to Load Balancers.

Step 9 – Follow the instructions to assign security groups to load balancers and click Next.

Step 10 – A new pop-up will open having health checkup configuration details with default values. Values can be set on our own, however these are optional. Click on Next: Add EC2 Instances.

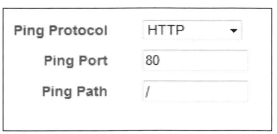

Ping Protocol	HTTP ▾
Ping Port	80
Ping Path	/

Step 11 – A pop-up window will open having information about instances like registered instances, add instances to load balancers by selecting ADD EC2 Instance option and fill the information required. Click Add Tags.

Step 12 – Adding tags to your load balancer is optional. To add tags click the Add Tags Page and fill the details such as key, value to the tag. Then choose Create Tag option. Click Review and Create button.

A review page opens on which we can verify the setting. We can even change the settings by choosing the edit link.

Step 13 – Click Create to create your load balancer and then click the Close button.

How to Delete a Load Balancer?

Step 1 – Go to Amazon EC2 console using this link – https://console.aws.amazon.com/ec2/.

Step 2 – Choose Load Balancers option from the navigation pane.

Step 3 – Select Load balancer and click the Action button.

Step 4 – Click the Delete button. An alert window will appear, click the Yes, Delete button.

Amazon Web Services - WorkSpaces

Amazon WorkSpaces is a fully managed desktop computing service in the cloud that allows its customers to provide cloud-based desktops to their end-users. Through this the end users can access the documents, applications, and resources using devices of their choice such as laptops, iPad, Kindle Fire, or Android tablets. This service was launched to meet its customers rising demand for Cloud based 'Desktop as a Service' (DaaS).

How It Works?

Each WorkSpace is a persistent Windows Server 2008 R2 instance that looks like Windows 7, hosted on the AWS cloud. Desktops are streamed to users via PCoIP and the data backed up will be taken on every 12 hours by default.

User Requirements

An Internet connection with TCP and UDP open ports is required at the user's end. They have to download a free Amazon WorkSpaces client application for their device.

How to Create Amazon Workspaces?

Step 1 – Create and configure the VPC. (This we will discuss in detail in the VPC chapter.)

Step 2 – Create an AD Directory using the following steps.

- Use the following link to open Amazon WorkSpace Console – https://console.aws.amazon.com/workspaces/
- Select Directories, then Setup Directory in the navigation panel.
- A new page will open. Select Create Simple AD button, then fill the required details.

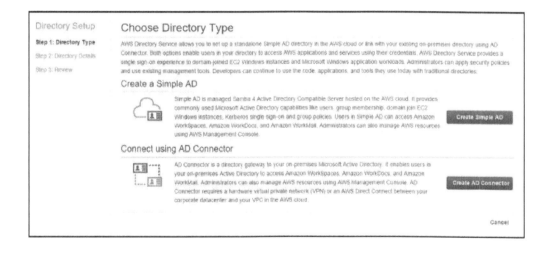

- In VPC section, fill the VPC details and select Next step.

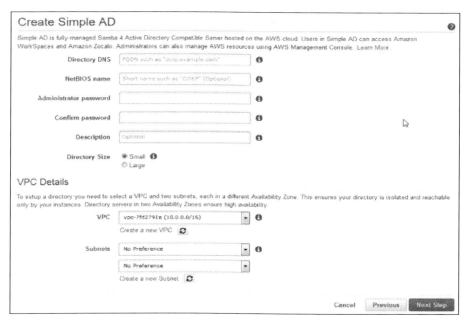

- A review page will open to review the information. Make changes if incorrect, then click the Create Simple AD button.

Step 3 – Create a WorkSpace using the following steps.

- Use the following link to open Amazon WorkSpace Console – https://console.aws.amazon.com/workspaces/
- Select Workspaces **and** then launch WorkSpaces option in the navigation panel.

- Select the cloud directory. Enable/disable WorkDocs for all users in this directory, then click the Yes, Next button.
- A new page will open. Fill the details for the new user and select the **Create Users** button. Once the user is added to the WorkSpace list, select Next.

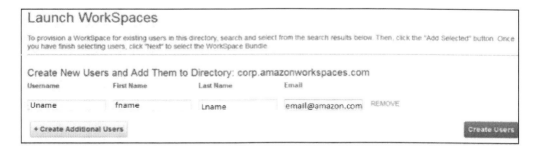

- Enter the number of bundles needed in the value field of WorkSpaces Bundles page, then select Next.
- A review page will open. Check the details and make changes if required. Select Launch WorkSpaces.

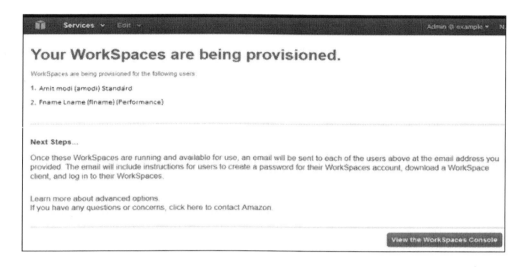

There will be a message to confirm the account, after which we can use WorkSpaces.

Step 4 – Test your WorkSpaces using the following steps.

Download and install the Amazon WorkSpaces client application using the following link – https://clients.amazonworkspaces.com/.

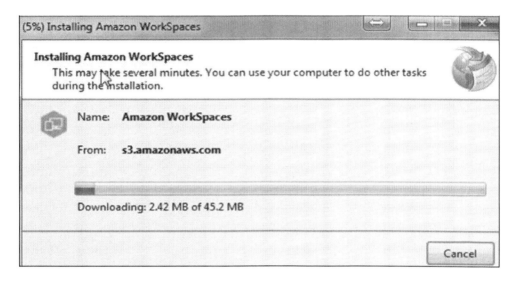

- Run the application. For the first time, we need to enter the registration code received in email and click Register.
- Connect to the WorkSpace by entering the user name and password for the user. Select Sign In.

Amazon Web Services - Lambda

AWS Lambda is a responsive cloud service that inspects actions within the application and responds by deploying the user-defined codes, known as **functions**. It automatically manages the compute resources across multiple availability zones and scales them when new actions are triggered.

AWS Lambda supports the code written in Java, Python and Node.js, and the service can launch processes in languages supported by Amazon Linux (includes Bash, Go & Ruby).

Following are some recommended tips while using AWS Lambda.

- Write your Lambda function code in a stateless style.
- Never declare any function variable outside the scope of the handler.
- Make sure to have a set of +rx **permissions** on your files in the uploaded ZIP to ensure Lambda can execute code on your behalf.
- Delete old Lambda functions when no longer required.

How to Configure AWS Lambda?

Follow these steps to configure AWS Lambda for the first time.

Step 1 – Sign in to AWS account.

Step 2 – Select Lambda from AWS services section.

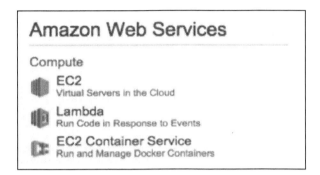

Step 3 – Select a Blueprint (optional) and click the Skip button.

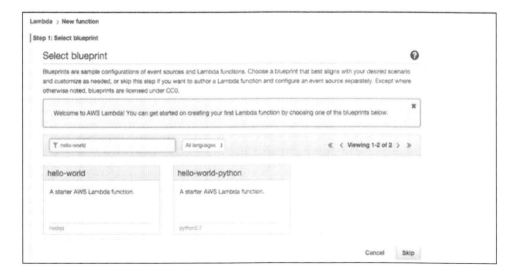

Step 4 – Provide the necessary details to create a **Lambda function** as shown in the following screenshot and paste the Node.js code that will be triggered automatically whenever a new item is added in DynamoDB. Select all the required permissions.

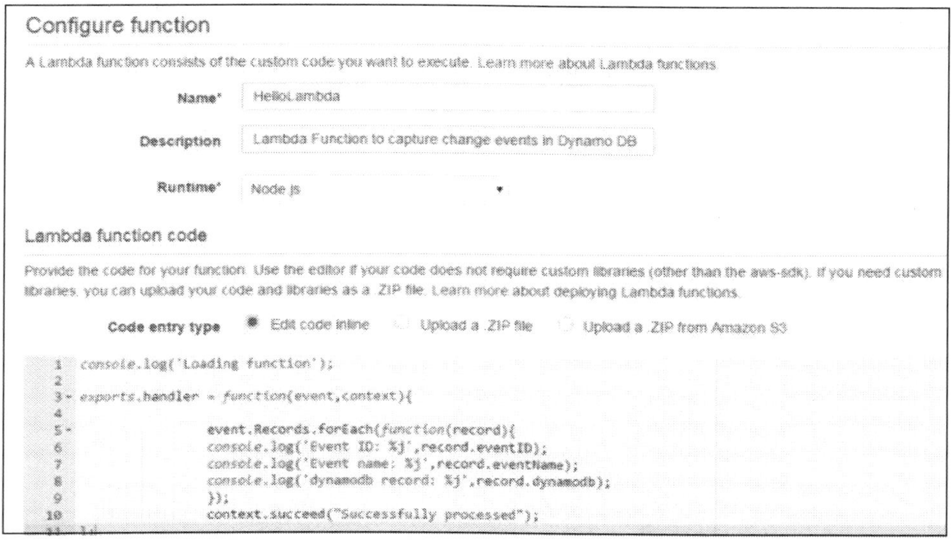

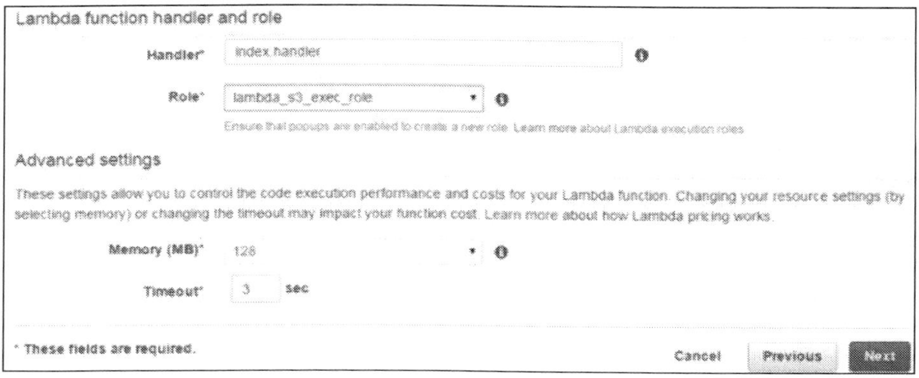

Step 5 – Click the Next button and verify your details.

Step 6 – Click the Create Function button.

Now, when we select the Lambda service and select the Event Sources tab, there will be no records. Add at least one source to the Lambda function to work. Here, we are adding DynamoDB Table to it.

We have created a table using DynamoDB (we will discuss this in detail in DynamoDB chapter).

Step 7 – Select the stream tab and associate it with the Lambda function.

You will see this entry in Event Sources Tab of Lambda Service page.

Step 8 – Add some entries into the table. When the entry gets added and saved, then Lambda service should trigger the function. It can be verified using the Lambda logs.

Step 9 – To view logs, select the Lambda service and click the Monitoring tab. Then click the View Logs in CloudWatch.

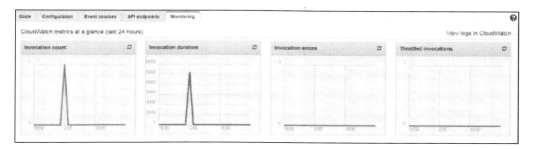

Benefits of AWS Lambda

Following are some of the benefits of using Lambda tasks —

- Lambda tasks need not to be registered like Amazon SWF activity types.
- We can use any existing Lambda functions that you've already defined in workflows.
- Lambda functions are called directly by Amazon SWF; there is no need design a program to implement and execute them.
- Lambda provides us the metrics and logs for tracking function executions.

-

AWS Lambda Limits

Following are the three types of Lambda limits.

Throttle Limit

The throttle limit is 100 concurrent Lambda function executions per account and is applied to the total concurrent executions across all functions within a same region.

The formula to calculate the number of concurrent executions for a function = (average duration of the function execution) X (number of requests or events processed by AWS Lambda).

When throttle limit is reached, then it returns a throttling error having an error code 429. After 15-30 minute you can start work again. The throttle limit can be increased by contacting AWS support center.

Resources Limit

The following table shows the list of resources limits for a Lambda function.

Resource	Default Limit
Ephemeral disk capacity ("/tmp" space)	512 MB
Number of file descriptors	1,024
Number of processes and threads (combined total)	1,024

Maximum execution duration per request	300 seconds
Invoke request body payload size	6 MB
Invoke response body payload size	6 MB

Service Limit

The following table shows the list of services limits for deploying a Lambda function.

Item	Default Limit
Lambda function deployment package size (.zip/.jar file)	50 MB
Size of code/dependencies that you can zip into a deployment package (uncompressed zip/jar size)	250 MB
Total size of all the deployment packages that can be uploaded per region	1.5 GB

Number of unique event sources of the Scheduled Event source type per account	50
Number of unique Lambda functions you can connect to each Scheduled Event	5

For latest updated limit structure & more information, visit – https://docs.aws.amazon.com/lambda/latest/dg/limits.html/

- Now WorkSpace desktop is displayed. Open this link http://aws.amazon.com/workspaces/ on THE web browser. Navigate and verify that the page can be viewed.
- A message saying "Congratulations! Your Amazon WorkSpaces cloud directory has been created, and your first WorkSpace is working correctly and has Internet access" will be received.

Amazon WorkSpaces Features

Network Health Check-Up

This AWS WorkSpaces feature verifies if the network and Internet connections are working, checks if WorkSpaces and their associated registration services are accessible, checks if the port 4172 is open for UDP and TCP access or not.

Client Reconnect

This AWS WorkSpaces feature allows the users to access to their WorkSpace without entering their credentials every time when they disconnect. The application installed at the client's device saves an access token in a secure store, which is valid for 12 hours and uses to authenticate the right user. Users click on the Reconnect button on the application to get access on their WorkSpace. Users can disable this feature any time.

Auto Resume Session

This AWS WorkSpaces feature allows the client to resume a session that was disconnected due to any reason in network connectivity within 20 minutes (by default and can be extended for 4 hours). Users can disable this feature any time in group policy section.

Console Search

This feature allows Administrators to search for WorkSpaces by their user name, bundle type, or directory.

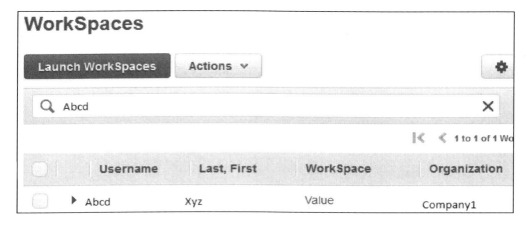

Benefits of Amazon WorkSpaces

- **Easy to set up** – Customers can choose AWS WorkSpaces plans of their choice and provide requirements such as CPU type, memory, storage and applications, and number of desktops.
- **Choice of devices and applications** – Customers can install Amazon WorkSpace application on their device (Laptops, iPads, Tablets) free of cost and can choose applications from the available list.
- **Cost-effective** – Amazon WorkSpaces require no upfront commitment and the customers pay as they customize their desktop, on a monthly basis.

Amazon Web Services - Virtual Private Cloud

Amazon Virtual Private Cloud (VPC) allows the users to use AWS resources in a virtual network. The users can customize their virtual networking environment as they like, such as selecting own IP address range, creating subnets, and configuring route tables and network gateways.

The list of AWS services that can be used with Amazon VPC are —

- Amazon EC2
- Amazon Route 53
- Amazon WorkSpaces
- Auto Scaling
- Elastic Load Balancing
- AWS Data Pipeline
- Elastic Beanstalk
- Amazon Elastic Cache
- Amazon EMR
- Amazon OpsWorks
- Amazon RDS
- Amazon Redshift

How to Use Amazon VPC?

Following are the steps to create VPC.

Create VPC

Step 1 — Open the Amazon VPC console by using the following link — https://console.aws.amazon.com/vpc/

Step 2 — Select creating the VPC option on the right side of the navigation bar. Make sure that the same region is selected as for other services.

Step 3 — Click the start VPC wizard option, then click VPC with single public subnet option on the left side.

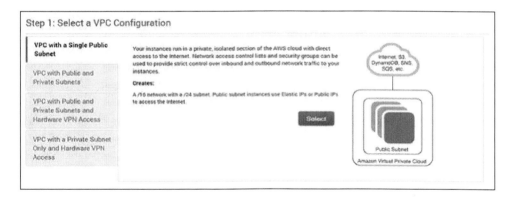

Step 4 – A configuration page will open. Fill in the details like VPC name, subnet name and leave the other fields as default. Click the Create VPC button.

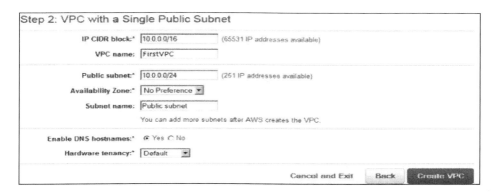

Step 5 – A dialog box will open, showing the work in progress. When it is completed, select the OK button.

The Your VPCs page opens which shows a list of available VPCs. The setting of VPC can be changed here.

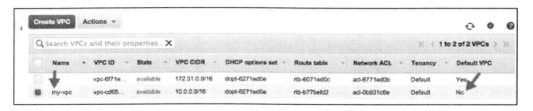

Select/Create VPC Group

Step 1 – Open the Amazon VPC console by using the following link – https://console.aws.amazon.com/vpc/

Step 2 – Select the security groups option in the navigation bar, then choose create security group option.

Step 3 – A form will open, enter the details like group name, name tag, etc. Select ID of your VPC from VPC menu, then select the Yes, create button.

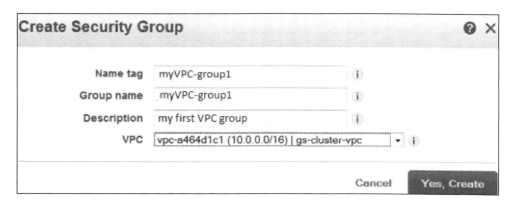

Step 4 – The list of groups opens. Select the group name from the list and set rules. Then click the Save button.

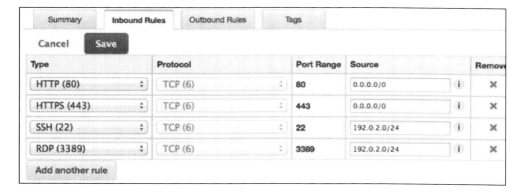

Launch Instance into VPC

Step 1 – Open the Amazon VPC console using the following link – https://console.aws.amazon.com/vpc/

Step 2 – Select the same region as while creating VPC and security group.

Step 3 – Now select the Launch Instance option in the navigation bar.

Step 4 – A page opens. Choose the AMI which is to be used.

Step 5 – A new page opens. Choose an Instance Type and select the hardware configuration. Then select **Next: Configure Instance Details**.

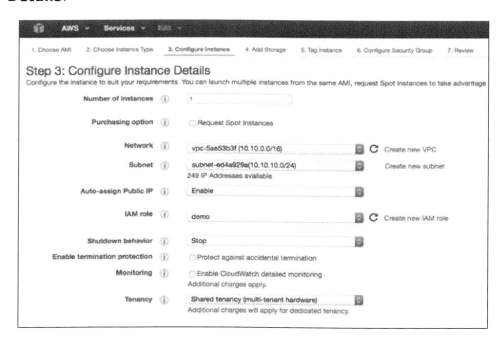

Step 6 – Select the recently created VPC from the Network list, and the subnet from the Subnet list. Leave the other settings as default and click Next till the Tag Instance page.

Step 7 – On the Tag Instance page, tag the instance with the Name tag. This helps to identify your instance from the list of multiple instances. Click Next: Configure Security Group.

Step 8 – On the Configure Security Group page, select the recently created group from the list. Then, select Review and Launch button.

Step 9 – On the Review Instance Launch page, check your instance details, then select Launch.

Step 10 – A dialog box appears. Choose the option Select an existing key pair or create a new key pair, then click the Launch Instances button.

Step 11 – The confirmation page open which shows all the details related to instances.

Assign Elastic IP Address to VPC Instances

Step 1 – Open the Amazon VPC console using the following link –
https://console.aws.amazon.com/vpc/

Step 2 – Select Elastic IP's option in the navigation bar.

Step 3 – Select Allocate New Address. Then select Yes, Allocate button.

Step 4 – Select your Elastic IP address from the list, then select Actions, and then click the Associate Address button.

Step 5 – A dialog box will open. First select the Instance from the Associate with list. Then select your instance from the Instance list. Finally click the Yes, Associate button.

Delete a VPC

There are several steps to delete VPC without losing any resources associated with it. Following are the steps to delete a VPC.

Step 1 – Open the Amazon VPC console using the following link – https://console.aws.amazon.com/vpc/

Step 2 – Select Instances option in the navigation bar.

Step 3 – Select the Instance from the list, then select the Actions → Instance State → Terminate button.

Step 4 – A new dialog box opens. Expand the Release attached Elastic IPs section, and select the checkbox next to the Elastic IP address. Click the Yes, Terminate button.

Step 5 – Again open the Amazon VPC console using the following link – https://console.aws.amazon.com/vpc/

Step 6 – Select the VPC from the navigation bar. Then select Actions & finally click the Delete VPC button.

Step 7 — A confirmation message appears. Click the Yes, Delete button.

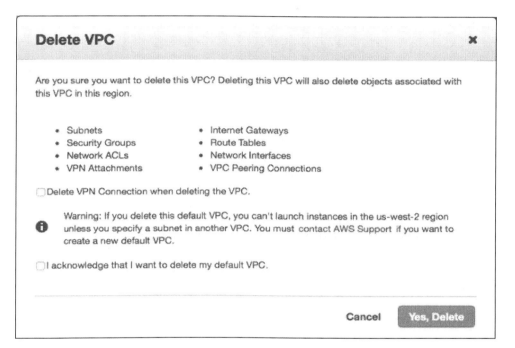

Features of VPC

- **Many connectivity options** – There are various connectivity options that exist in Amazon VPC.
  - Connect VPC directly to the Internet via public subnets.
  - Connect to the Internet using Network Address Translation via private subnets.
  - Connect securely to your corporate datacenter via encrypted IPsec hardware VPN connection.
  - Connect privately to other VPCs in which we can share resources across multiple virtual networks through AWS account.
  - Connect to Amazon S3 without using an internet gateway and have good control over S3 buckets, its user requests, groups, etc.
  - Combine connection of VPC and datacenter is possible by configuring Amazon VPC route tables to direct all traffic to its destination.
- **Easy to use** – Ease of creating a VPC in very simple steps by selecting network set-ups as per requirement. Click "Start VPC Wizard", then Subnets, IP ranges, route tables, and security groups will be automatically created.
- **Easy to backup data** – Periodically backup data from the datacenter into Amazon EC2 instances by using Amazon EBS volumes.
- **Easy to extend network using Cloud** – Move applications, launch additional web servers and increase storage capacity by connecting it to a VPC.

Amazon Web Services - Route 53

Amazon Route 53 is a highly available and scalable Domain Name System (DNS) web service. It is designed for developers and corporates to route the end users to Internet applications by translating human readable names like www.mydomain.com, into the numeric IP addresses like 192.0.2.1 that computers use to connect to each other.

How to Configure Amazon Route 53?

Following are the steps to configure Route 53.

Step 1 – Open the Amazon Route 53 console using this link – https://console.aws.amazon.com/route53/.

Step 2 – Click create hosted zone option on the top left corner of the navigation bar.

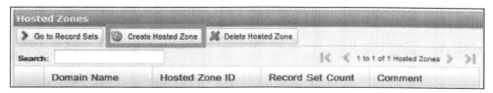

Step 3 − A form page opens. Provide the required details such as domain name and comments, then click the Create button.

Create Hosted Zone

A hosted zone is a container that holds information about how you want to route traffic for a domain, such as example.com, and its subdomains.

Domain Name:
myDomain.com

Comment:
Demo

Type:
Private Hosted Zone for Amazon VPC ▼

A private hosted zone determines how traffic is routed within an Amazon VPC. Your resources are not accessible outside the VPC. You can use any domain name.

VPC Id:
vpc-dc8899sf ▼

Create

Step 4 – Hosted zone for the domain will be created. There will be four DNS endpoints called delegation set and these endpoints must be updated in the domain names Nameserver settings.

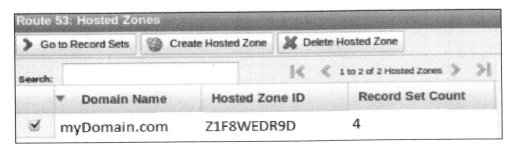

Step 5 – If it is godaddy.com then select domain's control panel and update the Route 53 DNS endpoints. Delete the rest default values. It will take 2-3 minutes to update.

Step 6 – Go back to Route 53 console and select the go to record sets option. This will show you the list of record sets. By default, there are two record sets of type NS & SOA.

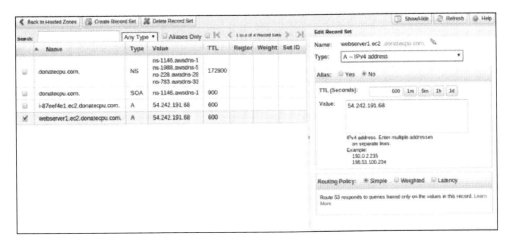

Step 7 – To create your record set, select the create record set option. Fill the required details such as: Name, Type, Alias, TTL seconds, Value, Routing policy, etc. Click the Save record set button.

Step 8 – Create one more record set for some other region so that there are two record sets with the same domain name pointing to different IP addresses with your selected routing policy.

Once completed, the user requests will be routed based on the network policy.

Features of Route 53

- Easy to register your domain — We can purchase all level of domains like .com, .net, .org, etc. directly from Route 53.
- **Highly reliable** — Route 53 is built using AWS infrastructure. Its distributed nature towards DNS servers help to ensure a consistent ability to route applications of end users.
- **Scalable** — Route 53 is designed in such a way that it automatically handles large volume queries without the user's interaction.
- **Can be used with other AWS Services** — Route 53 also works with other AWS services. It can be used to map domain names to our Amazon EC2 instances, Amazon S3 buckets, Amazon and other AWS resources.
- **Easy to use** — It is easy to sign-up, easy to configure DNS settings, and provides quick response to DNS queries.
- Health Check: Route 53 monitors the health of the application. If an outage is detected, then it automatically redirects the users to a healthy resource.
- **Cost-Effective** — Pay only for the domain service and the number of queries that the service answers for each domain.
- **Secure** — By integrating Route 53 with AWS (IAM), there is complete control over every user within the AWS account, such as deciding which user can access which part of Route 53.

Amazon Web Services - Direct Connect

AWS Direct Connect permits to create a private network connection from our network to AWS location. It uses 802.1q VLANs, which can be partitioned into multiple virtual interfaces to access public resources using the same connection. This results in reduced network cost and increased bandwidth. Virtual interfaces can be reconfigured at any time as per the requirement.

Requirements to Use AWS Direct Connect

Our network must meet one of the following conditions to use AWS Direct Connect −

- Our network should be in the AWS Direct Connect location. Visit this link to know about the available AWS Direct Connect locations https://aws.amazon.com/directconnect/.
- We should be working with an AWS Direct Connect partner who is a member of the AWS Partner Network (APN). Visit this link to know the list of AWS Direct Connect partners − https://aws.amazon.com/directconnect/
- Our service provider must be portable to connect to AWS Direct Connect.

Additionally, our network must meet the following necessary conditions −

- Connections to AWS Direct Connect requires single mode fiber, 1000BASE-LX (1310nm) for 1 gigabit Ethernet, or 10GBASE-LR

(1310nm) for 10 gigabit Ethernet. Auto Negotiation for the port must be disabled. Support for 802.1Q VLANs across these connections should be available.

• Network must support Border Gateway Protocol (BGP) and BGP MD5 authentication. Optionally, we may configure Bidirectional Forwarding Detection (BFD).

How to Configure AWS Direct Connect?

Following are the steps to configure AWS Direct Connect —

Step 1 — Open the AWS Direct Connect console using this link — https://console.aws.amazon.com/directconnect/

step 2 — Select AWS Direct Connect region from the navigation bar.

step 3 — Welcome page of AWS Direct Connect opens. Select Get Started with Direct Connect.

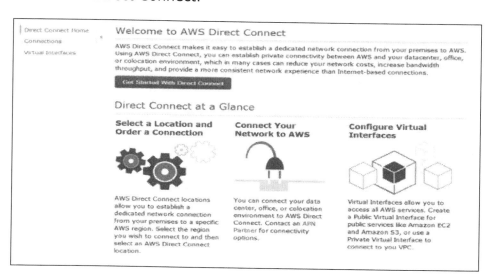

step 4 – Create a Connection dialog box opens up. Fill the required details and click the Create button.

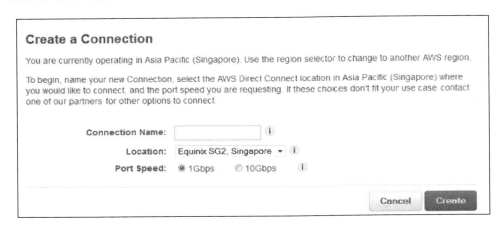

AWS will send an confirmation email within 72 hours to the authorized user.

Step 5 – Create a Virtual Interface using the following steps.

- Open AWS console page again.

- Select Connection in the navigation bar, then select Create Virtual Interface. Fill the required details and click the Continue button.

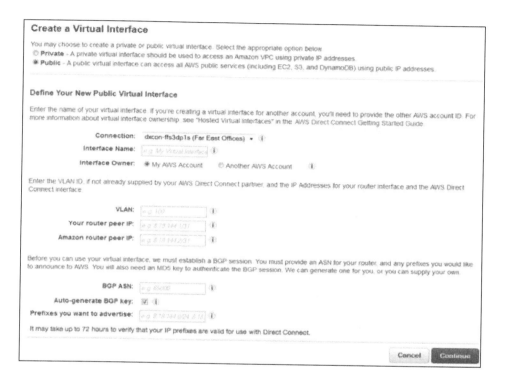

- Select Download Router Configuration, then click the Download button.

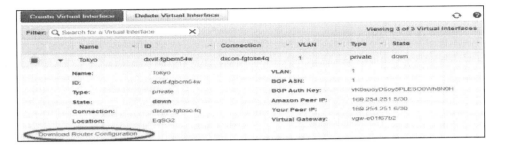

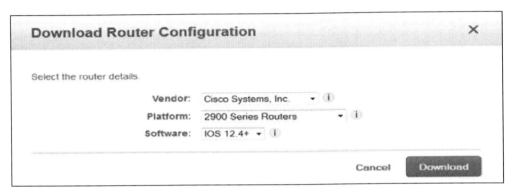

- Verify the Virtual Interface (optional). To verify the AWS Direct Connect connections use the following procedures.
- **To verify virtual interface connection to the AWS cloud** – Run traceroute and verify that the AWS Direct Connect identifier is in the network trace.
- **To verify virtual interface connection to Amazon VPC** – Use any pingable AMI and launch Amazon EC2 instance into the VPC that is attached to the virtual private gateway.
- When an instance is running, get its private IP address and ping the IP address to get a response.

Features of Direct Connect

- **Reduces bandwidth costs** – The cost gets reduced in both ways, i.e. it transfers the data to and from AWS directly. The data transferred over your dedicated connection is charged at reduced AWS Direct Connect data transfer rate rather than Internet data transfer rates.
- **Compatible with all AWS services** – AWS Direct Connect is a network service, supports all the AWS services that are accessible over the Internet, like Amazon S3, Amazon EC2, Amazon VPC, etc.
- **Private connectivity to Amazon VPC** – AWS Direct Connect can be used to establish a private virtual interface from our home-network to Amazon VPC directly with high bandwidth.
- **Elastic** – AWS Direct Connect provides 1 Gbps and 10 Gbps connections, having provision to make multiple connections as per requirement.
- **Easy and simple** – Easy to sign up on AWS Direct Connect using the AWS Management Console. Using this console, all the connections and virtual interfaces can be managed.

Amazon Web Services - Amazon S3

Amazon S3 (Simple Storage Service) is a scalable, high-speed, low-cost web-based service designed for online backup and archiving of data and application programs. It allows to upload, store, and download any type of files up to 5 GB in size. This service allows the subscribers to access the same systems that Amazon uses to run its own web sites. The subscriber has control over the accessibility of data, i.e. privately/publicly accessible.

How to Configure S3?

Following are the steps to configure a S3 account.

Step 1 — Open the Amazon S3 console using this link — https://console.aws.amazon.com/s3/home

Step 2 — Create a Bucket using the following steps.

* A prompt window will open. Click the Create Bucket button at the bottom of the page.

Welcome to Amazon Simple Storage Service

Amazon S3 is storage for the Internet. It is designed to make web-scale computing easier for developers.

Amazon S3 provides a simple web services interface that can be used to store and retrieve any amount of data, at any time, from anywhere on the web. It gives any developer access to the same highly scalable, reliable, secure, fast, inexpensive infrastructure that Amazon uses to run its own global network of web sites. The service aims to maximize benefits of scale and to pass those benefits on to developers.

You can read, write, and delete objects ranging in size from 1 byte to 5 terabytes each. The number of objects you can store is unlimited. Each object is stored in a bucket with a unique key that you assign.

Get started by simply creating a bucket and uploading a test object, for example a photo or .txt file.

Create Bucket

- Create a Bucket dialog box will open. Fill the required details and click the Create button.

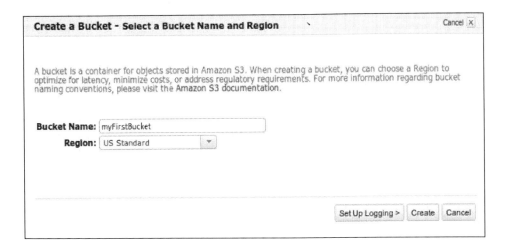

- The bucket is created successfully in Amazon S3. The console displays the list of buckets and its properties.

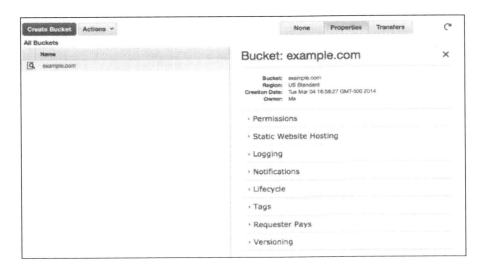

- Select the Static Website Hosting option. Click the radio button Enable website hosting and fill the required details.

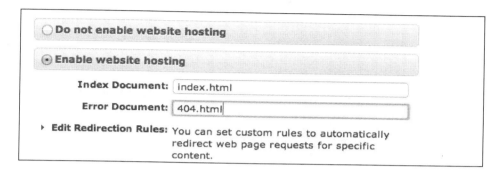

Step 3 — Add an Object to a bucket using the following steps.

- Open the Amazon S3 console using the following link — https://console.aws.amazon.com/s3/home
- Click the Upload button.

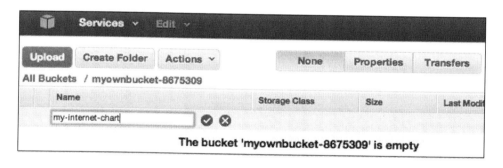

- Click the Add files option. Select those files which are to be uploaded from the system and then click the Open button.

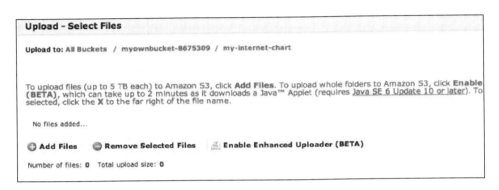

- Click the start upload button. The files will get uploaded into the bucket.

To open/download an object – In the Amazon S3 console, in the Objects & Folders list, right-click on the object to be opened/downloaded. Then, select the required object.

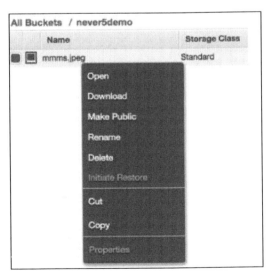

How to Move S3 Objects?

Following are the steps to move S3 objects.

step 1 – Open Amazon S3 console.

step 2 – Select the files & folders option in the panel. Right-click on the object that is to be moved and click the Cut option.

Amazon Web Services - Elastic Block Store

Amazon Elastic Block Store (EBS) is a block storage system used to store persistent data. Amazon EBS is suitable for EC2 instances by providing highly available block level storage volumes. It has three types of volume, i.e. General Purpose (SSD), Provisioned IOPS (SSD), and Magnetic. These three volume types differ in performance, characteristics, and cost.

EBS Volume Types

Following are the three types.

EBS General Purpose (SSD)

This volume type is suitable for small and medium workloads like Root disk EC2 volumes, small and medium database workloads, frequently logs accessing workloads, etc. By default, SSD supports 3 IOPS (Input Output Operations per Second)/GB means 1 GB volume will give 3 IOPS, and 10 GB volume will give 30 IOPS. Its storage capacity of one volume ranges from 1 GB to 1 TB. The cost of one volume is $0.10 per GB for one month.

Provisioned IOPS (SSD)

This volume type is suitable for the most demanding I/O intensive, transactional workloads and large relational, EMR and Hadoop workloads, etc. By default, IOPS SSD supports 30 IOPS/GB means 10GB volume will give 300 IOPS. Its storage capacity of one volume ranges from 10GB to 1TB. The cost of one volume is $0.125 per GB for one month for provisioned storage and $0.10 per provisioned IOPS for one month.

EBS Magnetic Volumes

It was formerly known as standard volumes. This volume type is suitable for ideal workloads like infrequently accessing data, i.e. data backups for recovery, logs storage, etc. Its storage capacity of one volume ranges from 10GB to 1TB. The cost of one volume is $0.05 per GB for one month for provisioned storage and $0. 05 per million I/O requests.

Volumes Attached to One Instance

Each account will be limited to 20 EBS volumes. For a requirement of more than 20 EBS volumes, contact Amazon's Support team. We can attach up to 20 volumes on a single instance and each volume ranges from 1GB to 1TB in size.

In EC2 instances, we store data in local storage which is available till the instance is running. However, when we shut down the instance, the data gets lost. Thus, when we need to save anything, it is advised to save it on Amazon EBS, as we can access and read the EBS volumes anytime, once we attach the file to an EC2 instance.

Amazon EBS Benefits

- **Reliable and secure storage** – Each of the EBS volume will automatically respond to its Availability Zone to protect from component failure.
- **Secure** – Amazon's flexible access control policies allows to specify who can access which EBS volumes. Access control plus encryption offers a strong defense-in-depth security strategy for data.
- **Higher performance** – Amazon EBS uses SSD technology to deliver data results with consistent I/O performance of application.
- **Easy data backup** – Data backup can be saved by taking point-in-time snapshots of Amazon EBS volumes.

How to Set Up Amazon EBS?

Step 1 – Create Amazon EBS volume using the following steps.

- Open the Amazon EC2 console.
- Select the region in the navigation bar where the volume is to be created.
- In the navigation pane, select Volumes, then select Create Volume.
- Provide the required information like Volume Type list, Size, IOPS, Availability zone, etc. then click the Create button.

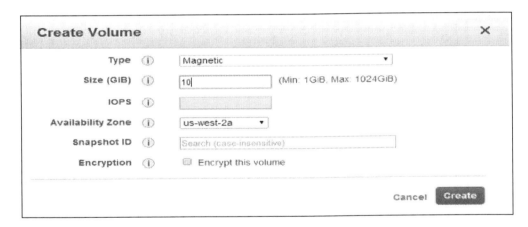

The volume names can be seen in the volumes list.

Step 2 – Store EBS Volume from a snapshot using the following steps.

- Repeat the above 1 to 4 steps to create volume.

- Type snapshot ID in the Snapshot ID field from which the volume is to be restored and select it from the list of suggested options.
- If there is requirement for more storage, change the storage size in the Size field.
- Select the Yes Create button.

Step 3 – Attach EBS Volume to an Instance using the following steps.

- Open the Amazon EC2 console.
- Select Volumes in the navigation pane. Choose a volume and click the Attach Volume option.

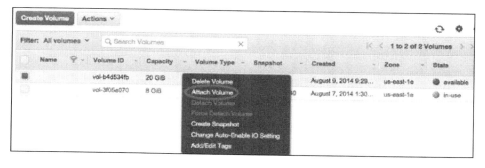

- An Attach Volume dialog box will open. Enter the name/ID of instance to attach the volume in the Instance field or select it from the list of suggestion options.
- Click the Attach button.

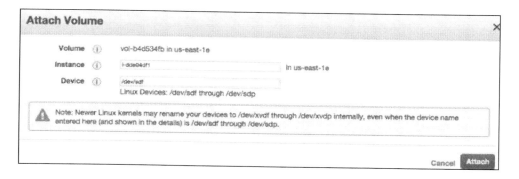

- Connect to instance and make the volume available.

Step 4 – Detach a volume from Instance.

- First, use the command /dev/sdh in cmd to unmount the device.
- Open the Amazon EC2 console.
- In the navigation pane, select the Volumes option.
- Choose a volume and click the Detach Volumes option.

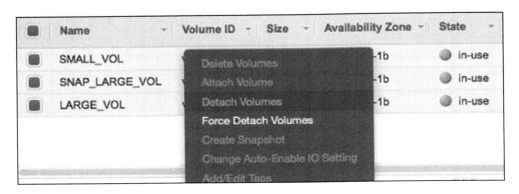

- A confirmation dialog box opens. Click the Yes, Detach button to confirm.

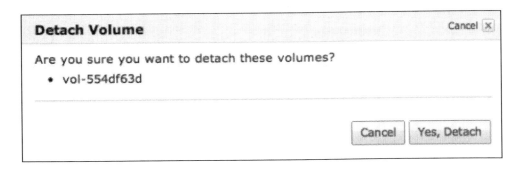

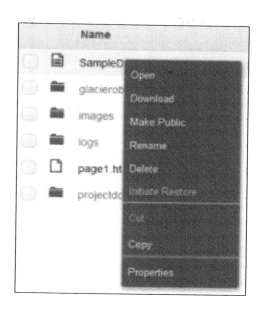

step 3 – Open the location where we want this object. Right-click on the folder/bucket where the object is to be moved and click the Paste into option.

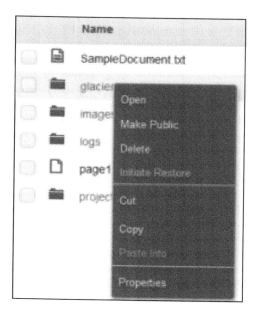

How to Delete an Object?

Step 1 – Open Amazon S3.

Step 2 – Select the files & folders option in the panel. Right-click on the object that is to be deleted. Select the delete option.

Step 3 – A pop-up window will open for confirmation. Click Ok.

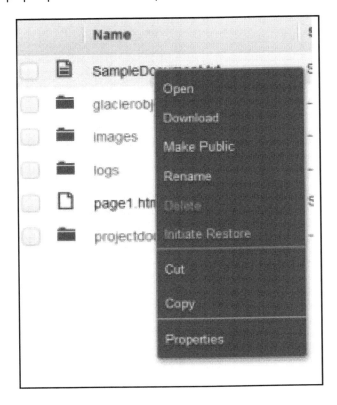

How to Empty a Bucket?

Step 1 – Open Amazon S3 console.

Step 2 – Right-click on the bucket that is to be emptied and click the empty bucket option.

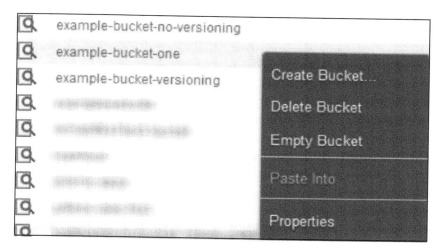

Step 3 – A confirmation message will appear on the pop-up window. Read it carefully and click the **Empty bucket** button to confirm.

Empty bucket

Deleting all objects (including older versions if applicable) in this bucket cannot be undone. Are you sure you want to empty **example-bucket-one**?

Type the name of the bucket to confirm deletion

Bucket name

Cancel   Empty bucket

Amazon S3 Features

- **Low cost and Easy to Use** — Using Amazon S3, the user can store a large amount of data at very low charges.
- **Secure** — Amazon S3 supports data transfer over SSL and the data gets encrypted automatically once it is uploaded. The user has complete control over their data by configuring bucket policies using AWS IAM.
- **Scalable** — Using Amazon S3, there need not be any worry about storage concerns. We can store as much data as we have and access it anytime.
- **Higher performance** — Amazon S3 is integrated with Amazon CloudFront, that distributes content to the end users with low latency and provides high data transfer speeds without any minimum usage commitments.
- **Integrated with AWS services** — Amazon S3 integrated with AWS services include Amazon CloudFront, Amazon CLoudWatch, Amazon Kinesis, Amazon RDS, Amazon Route 53, Amazon VPC, AWS Lambda, Amazon EBS, Amazon Dynamo DB, etc.

Amazon Web Services - Storage Gateway

AWS Storage Gateway provides integration between the on-premises IT environment and the AWS storage infrastructure. The user can store data in the AWS cloud for scalable, data security features and cost-efficient storage.

AWS Gateway offers two types of storage, i.e. volume based and tape based.

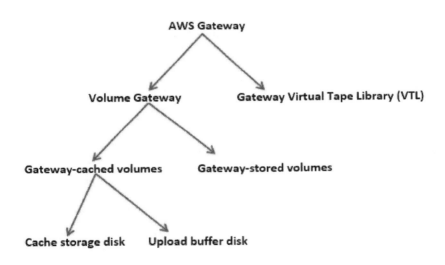

Volume Gateways

This storage type provides cloud-backed storage volumes which can be mount as Internet Small Computer System Interface (iSCSI) devices from on-premises application servers.

Gateway-cached Volumes

AWS Storage Gateway stores all the on-premises application data in a storage volume in Amazon S3. Its storage volume ranges from 1GB to 32 TB and up to 20 volumes with a total storage of 150TB. We can attach these volumes with iSCSI devices from on-premises application servers. It is of two categories —

Cache Storage Disk

Every application requires storage volumes to store their data. This storage type is used to initially store data when it is to be written to the storage volumes in AWS. The data from the cache storage disk is waiting to be uploaded to Amazon S3 from the upload buffer. The cache storage disk keeps the most recently accessed data for low-latency access. When the application needs data, the cache storage disk is first checked before checking Amazon S3.

There are few guidelines to determine the amount of disk space to be allocated for cache storage. We should allocate at least 20% of the existing file store size as cache storage. It should be more than the upload buffer.

Upload buffer disk — This type of storage disk is used to store the data before it is uploaded to Amazon S3 over SSL connection. The storage gateway uploads the data from the upload buffer over an SSL connection to AWS.

Snapshots – Sometimes we need to back up storage volumes in Amazon S3. These backups are incremental and are known as **snapshots**. The snapshots are stored in Amazon S3 as Amazon EBS snapshots. Incremental backup means that a new snapshot is backing up only the data that has changed since the last snapshot. We can take snapshots either at a scheduled interval or as per the requirement.

Gateway-stored Volumes

When the Virtual Machine (VM) is activated, gateway volumes are created and mapped to the on-premises direct-attached storage disks. Hence, when the applications write/read the data from the gateway storage volumes, it reads and writes the data from the mapped on-premises disk.

A gateway-stored volume allows to store primary data locally and provides on-premises applications with low-latency access to entire datasets. We can mount them as iSCSI devices to the on-premises application servers. It ranges from 1 GB to 16 TB in size and supports up to 12 volumes per gateway with a maximum storage of 192 TB.

Gateway-Virtual Tape Library (VTL)

This storage type provides a virtual tape infrastructure that scales seamlessly with your business needs and eliminates the operational burden of provisioning, scaling, and maintaining a physical tape infrastructure. Each gateway-VTL is preconfigured with media changer and tape drives, that are available with the existing client backup applications as iSCSI devices. Tape cartridges can be added later as required to archive the data.

Few terms used in Architecture are explained below.

Virtual Tape – Virtual tape is similar to a physical tape cartridge. It is stored in the AWS cloud. We can create virtual tapes in two ways:

118

by using AWS Storage Gateway console or by using AWS Storage Gateway API. The size of each virtual tape is from 100 GB to 2.5 TB. The size of one gateway is up to 150 TB and can have maximum 1500 tapes at a time.

Virtual Tape Library (VTL) – Each gateway-VTL comes with one VTL. VTL is similar to a physical tape library available on-premises with tape drives. The gateway first stores data locally, then asynchronously uploads it to virtual tapes of VTL.

Tape Drive – A VTL tape drive is similar to a physical tape drive that can perform I/O operations on tape. Each VTL consists of 10 tape drives that are used for backup applications as iSCSI devices.

Media Changer – A VTL media changer is similar to a robot that moves tapes around in a physical tape library's storage slots and tape drives. Each VTL comes with one media changer that is used for backup applications as iSCSI device.

Virtual Tape Shelf (VTS) – A VTS is used to archive tapes from gateway VTL to VTS and vice-a-versa.

Archiving Tapes – When the backup software ejects a tape, the gateway moves the tape to the VTS for storage. It is used data archiving and backups.

Retrieving Tapes – Tapes archived to the VTS cannot be read directly so to read an archived tape, we need to retrieve the tape from gateway VTL either by using the AWS Storage Gateway console or by using the AWS Storage Gateway API.

Amazon Web Services - CloudFront

CloudFront is a **CDN (Content Delivery Network)**. It retrieves data from Amazon S3 bucket and distributes it to multiple datacenter locations. It delivers the data through a network of data centers called **edge locations**. The nearest edge location is routed when the user requests for data, resulting in lowest latency, low network traffic, fast access to data, etc.

How AWS CloudFront Delivers the Content?

AWS CloudFront delivers the content in the following steps.

Step 1 – The user accesses a website and requests an object to download like an image file.

Step 2 – DNS routes your request to the nearest CloudFront edge location to serve the user request.

Step 3 – At edge location, CloudFront checks its cache for the requested files. If found, then returns it to the user otherwise does the following –

- First CloudFront compares the request with the specifications and forwards it to the applicable origin server for the corresponding file type.
- The origin servers send the files back to the CloudFront edge location.
- As soon as the first byte arrives from the origin, CloudFront starts forwarding it to the user and adds the files to the cache in the edge location for the next time when someone again requests for the same file.

Step 4 – The object is now in an edge cache for 24 hours or for the provided duration in file headers. CloudFront does the following –

- CloudFront forwards the next request for the object to the user's origin to check the edge location version is updated or not.
- If the edge location version is updated, then CloudFront delivers it to the user.

- If the edge location version is not updated, then origin sends the latest version to CloudFront. CloudFront delivers the object to the user and stores the latest version in the cache at that edge location.

Features of CloudFront

Fast – The broad network of edge locations and CloudFront caches copies of content close to the end users that results in lowering latency, high data transfer rates and low network traffic. All these make CloudFront fast.

Simple – It is easy to use.

Can be used with other AWS Services – Amazon CloudFront is designed in such a way that it can be easily integrated with other AWS services, like Amazon S3, Amazon EC2.

Cost-effective – Using Amazon CloudFront, we pay only for the content that you deliver through the network, without any hidden charges and no up-front fees.

Elastic – Using Amazon CloudFront, we need not worry about maintenance. The service automatically responds if any action is needed, in case the demand increases or decreases.

Reliable – Amazon CloudFront is built on Amazon's highly reliable infrastructure, i.e. its edge locations will automatically re-route the end users to the next nearest location, if required in some situations.

Global – Amazon CloudFront uses a global network of edge locations located in most of the regions.

How to Set Up AWS CloudFront?

AWS CloudFront can be set up using the following steps.

Step 1 – Sign in to AWS management console using the following link – https://console.aws.amazon.com/

Step 2 – Upload Amazon S3 and choose every permission public. (How to upload content to S3 bucket is discussed in chapter 14)

Step 3 – Create a CloudFront Web Distribution using the following steps.

- Open CloudFront console using the following link – https://console.aws.amazon.com/cloudfront/
- Click the Get Started button in the web section of Select a delivery method for your content page.

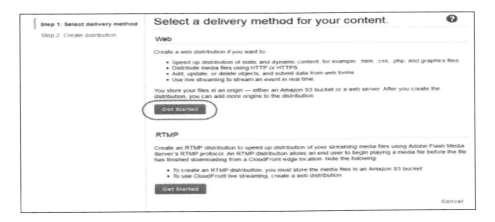

- **Create Distribution** page opens. Choose the Amazon S3 bucket created in the Origin Domain Name and leave the remaining fields as default.

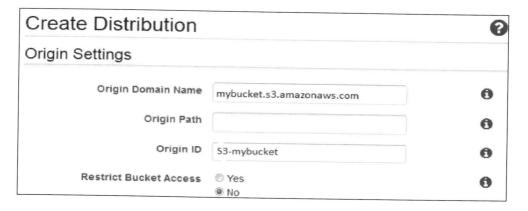

- Default Cache Behavior Settings page opens. Keep the values as default and move to the next page.
- A Distribution settings page opens. Fill the details as per your requirement and click the Create Distribution button.
- The Status column changes from In Progress to Deployed. Enable your distribution by selecting the Enable option. It will take around 15 minutes for the domain name to be available in the Distributions list.

Test the Links

After creating distribution, CloudFront knows the location of Amazon S3 server and the user knows the domain name associated with the distribution. However, we can also create a link to Amazon S3 bucket content with that domain name and have CloudFront serve it. This helps save a lot of time.

Following are the steps to link an object –

Step 1 – Copy the following HTML code to a new file and write the domain-name that CloudFront assigned to the distribution in the place of domain name. Write a file name of Amazon S3 bucket in the place of object-name.

```html
<html>
  <head>CloudFront                    Testing                    link</head>
  <body>
    <p>My                                                    Cludfront.</p>
    <p><img  src  =  "http://domain-name/object-name"  alt  =  "test
image"/>
  </body>
</html>
```

Step 2 – Save the text in a file with **.html** extension.

Step 3 – Open the web page in a browser to test the links to see if they are working correctly. If not, then crosscheck the settings.

AWS - Relational Database Service

Amazon RDS (Relational Database Service) is a fully-managed SQL database cloud service that allows to create and operate relational databases. Using RDS you can access your files and database anywhere in a cost-effective and highly scalable way.

Features of Amazon RDS

Amazon RDS has the following features —

- **Scalable** — Amazon RDS allows to scale the relational database by using AWS Management Console or RDS-specific API. We can increase or decrease your RDS requirements within minutes.
- **Host replacement** — Sometimes these situations occur when the hardware of Amazon RDS fails. There is no need to worry, it will be automatically replaced by Amazon.
- **Inexpensive** — Using Amazon RDS, we pay only for the resources we consume. There is no up-front and long-term commitment.
- **Secure** — Amazon RDS provides complete control over the network to access their database and their associated services.
- **Automatic backups** — Amazon RDS backs up everything in the database including transaction logs up to last five minutes and also manages automatic backup timings.
- **Software patching** — Automatically gets all the latest patches for the database software. We can also specify when the software should be patched using DB Engine Version Management.

How to Set Up Amazon RDS?

Step 1 – Login to AWS management console. Use the following link to open Amazon RDS console – https://console.aws.amazon.com/rds/

Step 2 – Select the region where the DB instance is to be created, at the top right corner of the Amazon RDS console.

Step 3 – Select Instances in the navigation pane, then click Launch DB Instance button.

Step 4 – The Launch DB Instance Wizard opens. Select the type of instance as required to launch and click the Select button.

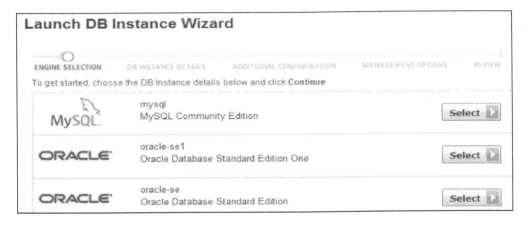

Step 5 – On the Specify DB Details page, provide the required details and click the Continue button.

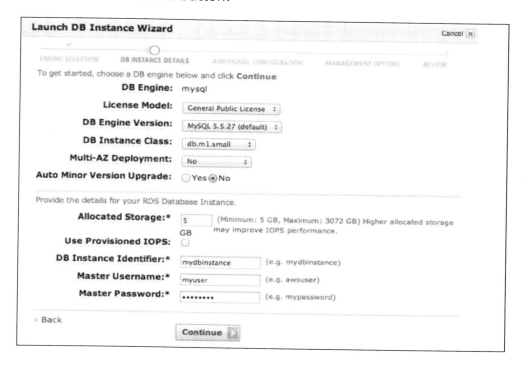

Step 6 – On the Additional configuration page, provide the additional information required to launch the MySQL DB instance and click the Continue button.

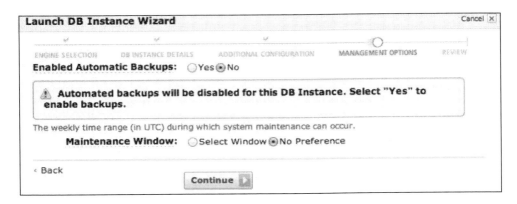

Step 7 – On Management options page, make the choices and click the Continue button.

Step 8 – On the Review page, verify the details and click the Launch DB Instance button.

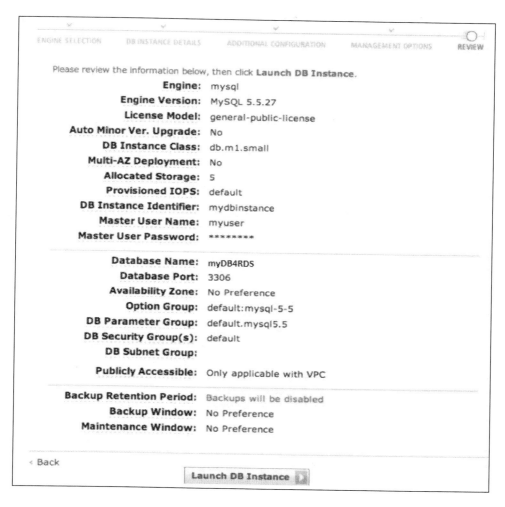

Now DB instance shows in the list of DB instances.

How to Connect Database to MySQL DB Instance?

Following are the steps to connect a database on MySQL DB instance —

Step 1 — Type the following command in the command prompt on a client computer to connect a database on MySQL DB instance (using the MySQL monitor).

Step 2 — Replace <myDBI> with DNS name of your DB instance, <myusername> with your master user-name & <mypassword> with your master password.

PROMPT>   mysql   -h   <myDBI>   -P   3306   -u   <myusername>   -p

After running the above command, the output looks like —

Welcome to the MySQL monitor. Commands end with ; or \g.
Your MySQL connection id is 350
Server version: 5.2.33-log MySQL Community Server (GPL)
Type 'help;' or '\h' for help. Type '\c' to clear the buffer.
mysql>

How to Delete a DB Instance?

After completing the task, we should delete the DB instance so will not be charged for it. Follow these steps to delete a DB instance −

Step 1 − Sign in to the AWS Management Console and use the following link to open the Amazon RDS console.

https://console.aws.amazon.com/rds/

Step 2 − In the DB Instances list, select the DB instances to be deleted.

Step 3 − Click the Instance Actions button and then select the Delete option from the dropdown menu.

Step 4 − Select No in the Create Final Snapshot.

Step 5 − Click the Yes, Delete to delete the DB instance.

Cost of Amazon RDS

When using Amazon RDS, pay only for only the usage without any minimum and setup charges. Billing is based on the following criteria —

- **Instance class** — Pricing is based on the class of the DB instance consumed.
- **Running time** — Price is calculated by the instance-hour, which is equivalent to a single instance running per hour.
- **Storage** — Bill is calculated as per the storage capacity plan chosen in terms of per GB.
- **I/O requests per month** — Billing structure also includes total number of storage I/O requests made in a billing cycle.
- **Backup storage** — There is no additional charges for backup storage up to 100% of database. This service is free only for active DB instances.

For latest updated price structure and other details, visit the following link — https://aws.amazon.com/rds/pricing/

Amazon Web Services - DynamoDB

Amazon DynamoDB is a fully managed NoSQL database service that allows to create database tables that can store and retrieve any amount of data. It automatically manages the data traffic of tables over multiple servers and maintains performance. It also relieves the customers from the burden of operating and scaling a distributed database. Hence, hardware provisioning, setup, configuration, replication, software patching, cluster scaling, etc. is managed by Amazon.

How to Run DynamoDB on Computer?

Following are the steps to set up DynamoDB.

Step 1 – Following are the steps to set up DynamoDB.

- Download DynamoDB (.jar file) using the following link. It supports multiple Operating Systems like Windows, Linux, Mac, etc.
- .tar.gz **format** – http://dynamodb-local.s3-website-us-west2.amazonaws.com/dynamodb_local_latest.tar.gz
- .zip **format** – http://dynamodb-local.s3-website-us-west2.amazonaws.com/dynamodb_local_latest.zip.
- Once download is complete, extract the contents and copy the extracted directory to a location wherever you want.
- Open the command prompt and navigate to the directory where you extracted DynamoDBLocal.jar, and execute the following command –

```
java -Djava.library.path=./DynamoDBLocal_lib -jar DynamoDBLocal.jar -sharedDb
```

- Now there is access to the build-in javaScript shell.

Step 2 – Create a Table using the following steps.

- Open AWS Management Console and select DynamoDB.

- Select the region where the table will be created and click the Create Table button.

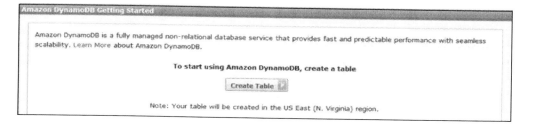

- Create Table window opens. Fill the details into their respective fields and click the Continue button.
- Finally, a review page opens where we can view details. Click the Create button.

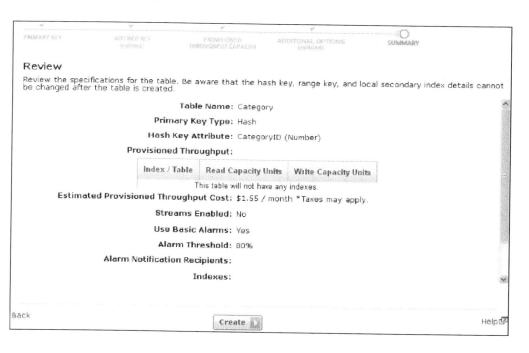

- Now the Table-name is visible in the in-to the list and Dynamo Table is ready to use.

▲ Name	Status	Hash Key
acct_table	ACTIVE	acctid
user_table	ACTIVE	last_name
users	ACTIVE	userid

Amazon DynamoDB Tables

Filter: [   ]   Explore Table | Create Table | Create Index | Modify Throughput | Delete Table

Benefits of Amazon DynamoDB

Managed **service** — Amazon DynamoDB is a managed service. There is no need to hire experts to manage NoSQL installation. Developers need not worry about setting up, configuring a distributed database cluster, managing ongoing cluster operations, etc. It handles all the complexities of scaling, partitions and re-partitions data over more machine resources to meet I/O performance requirements.

Scalable — Amazon DynamoDB is designed to scale. There is no need to worry about predefined limits to the amount of data each table can store. Any amount of data can be stored and retrieved. DynamoDB will spread automatically with the amount of data stored as the table grows.

Fast — Amazon DynamoDB provides high throughput at very low latency. As datasets grow, latencies remain stable due to the distributed nature of DynamoDB's data placement and request routing algorithms.

Durable and **h**ighly **a**vailable — Amazon DynamoDB replicates data over at least 3 different data centers' results. The system operates and serves data even under various failure conditions.

Flexible: Amazon DynamoDB allows creation of dynamic tables, i.e. the table can have any number of attributes, including multi-valued attributes.

Cost-effective: Payment is for what we use without any minimum charges. Its pricing structure is simple and easy to calculate.

Amazon Web Services - Redshift

Amazon Redshift is a fully managed data warehouse service in the cloud. Its datasets range from 100s of gigabytes to a petabyte. The initial process to create a data warehouse is to launch a set of compute resources called **nodes**, which are organized into groups called **cluster**. After that you can process your queries.

How to Set Up Amazon Redshift?

Following are the steps to set up Amazon Redshift.

Step 1 – Sign in and launch a Redshift Cluster using the following steps.

- Sign in to AWS Management console and use the following link to open Amazon Redshift console – https://console.aws.amazon.com/redshift/
- Select the region where the cluster is to be created using the Region menu on the top right side corner of the screen.
- Click the Launch Cluster button.

 Welcome to Amazon Redshift

You do not appear to have any clusters in the US East (N. Virginia) region.

Amazon Redshift is a fast and powerful, fully managed, petabyte-scale data warehouse service in the cloud. Amazon Redshift offers you fast query performance when analyzing virtually any size data set using the same SQL-based tools and business intelligence applications you use today. With a few clicks in the AWS Management Console, you can launch a Redshift cluster, starting with a few hundred gigabytes of data and scaling to a petabyte or more, for under $1,000 per terabyte per year.

Launch Cluster

- The Cluster Details page opens. Provide the required details and click the Continue button till the review page.

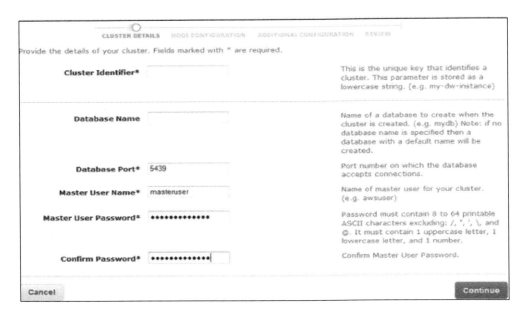

- A confirmation page opens. Click the Close button to finish so that cluster is visible in the Clusters list.

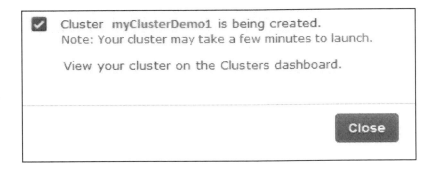

- Select the cluster in the list and review the Cluster Status information. The page will show Cluster status.

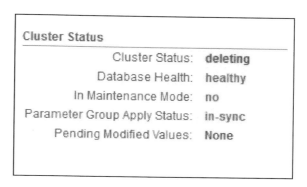

Step 2 – Configure security group to authorize client connections to the cluster. The authorizing access to Redshift depends on whether the client authorizes an EC2 instance or not.

Follow these steps to security group on EC2-VPC platform.

- Open Amazon Redshift Console and click Clusters on the navigation pane.
- Select the desired Cluster. Its Configuration tab opens.

- Click the Security group.
- Once the Security group page opens, click the Inbound tab.

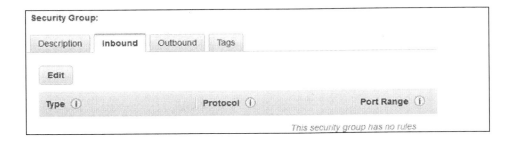

- Click the Edit button. Set the fields as shown below and click the Save button.
  - **Type** – Custom TCP Rule.
  - **Protocol** – TCP.
  - **Port Range** – Type the same port number used while launching the cluster. By-default port for Amazon Redshift is 5439.
  - **Source** – Select Custom IP, then type 0.0.0.0/0.

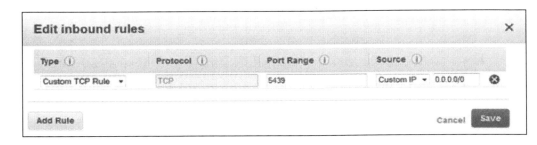

Step 3 – Connect to Redshift Cluster.

There are two ways to connect to Redshift Cluster – Directly or via SSL.

Following are the steps to connect directly.

- Connect the cluster by using a SQL client tool. It supports SQL client tools that are compatible with PostgreSQL JDBC or ODBC drivers.

- Use the following links to download — **JDBC** https://jdbc.postgresql.org/download/postgresql-8.4-703.jdbc4.jar
- **ODBC**

  https://ftp.postgresql.org/pub/odbc/versions/msi/psqlodbc_08_04_0200.zip   or

  http://ftp.postgresql.org/pub/odbc/versions/msi/psqlodbc_09_00_0101x64.zip for 64 bit machines
- Use the following steps to get the Connection String.
    - Open Amazon Redshift Console and select Cluster in the Navigation pane.
    - Select the cluster of choice and click the Configuration tab.
    - A page opens as shown in the following screenshot with JDBC URL under Cluster Database Properties. Copy the URL.

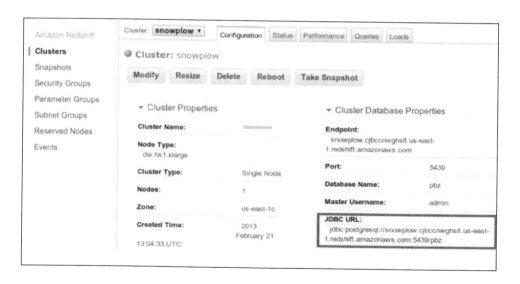

- Use the following steps to connect the Cluster with SQL Workbench/J.

145

- Open SQL Workbench/J.
- Select the File and click the Connect window.
- Select Create a new connection profile and fill the required details like name, etc.
- Click Manage Drivers and Manage Drivers dialog box opens.
- Click the Create a new entry button and fill the required details.

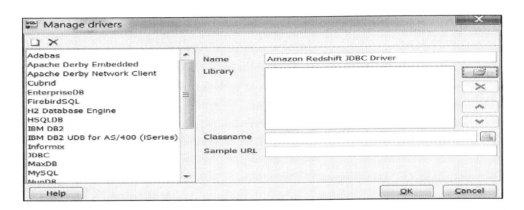

- Click the folder icon and navigate to the driver location. Finally, click the Open button.

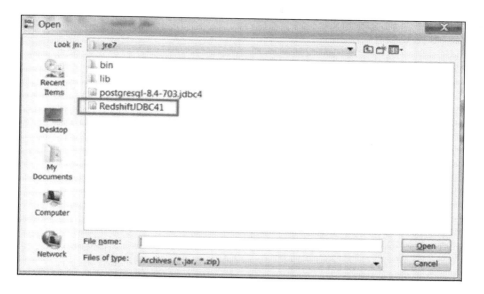

- Leave the Classname box and Sample URL box blank. Click OK.
- Choose the Driver from the list.
- In the URL field, paste the JDBC URL copied.
- Enter the username and password to their respective fields.

- Select the Autocommit box and click Save profile list.

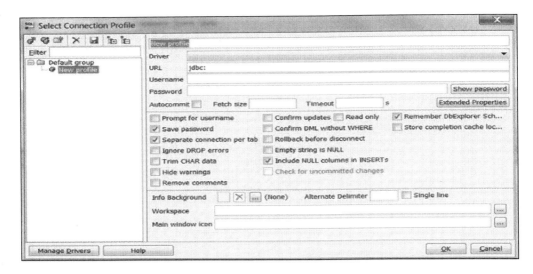

Features of Amazon Redshift

Following are the features of Amazon Redshift –

- **Supports VPC** – The users can launch Redshift within VPC and control access to the cluster through the virtual networking environment.
- **Encryption** – Data stored in Redshift can be encrypted and configured while creating tables in Redshift.
- **SSL** – SSL encryption is used to encrypt connections between clients and Redshift.
- **Scalable** – With a few simple clicks, the number of nodes can be easily scaled in your Redshift data warehouse as per requirement. It also allows to scale over storage capacity without any loss in performance.
- **Cost-effective** – Amazon Redshift is a cost-effective alternative to traditional data warehousing practices. There are no up-front costs, no long-term commitments and on-demand pricing structure.

Amazon Web Services - Kinesis

Amazon Kinesis is a managed, scalable, cloud-based service that allows real-time processing of streaming large amount of data per second. It is designed for real-time applications and allows developers to take in any amount of data from several sources, scaling up and down that can be run on EC2 instances.

It is used to capture, store, and process data from large, distributed streams such as event logs and social media feeds. After processing the data, Kinesis distributes it to multiple consumers simultaneously.

How to Use Amazon KCL?

It is used in situations where we require rapidly moving data and its continuous processing. Amazon Kinesis can be used in the following situations –

- **Data log and data feed intake** – We need not wait to batch up the data, we can push data to an Amazon Kinesis stream as soon as the data is produced. It also protects data loss in case of data producer fails. For example: System and application logs can be continuously added to a stream and can be available in seconds when required.
- **Real-time graphs** – We can extract graphs/metrics using Amazon Kinesis stream to create report results. We need not wait for data batches.
- **Real-time data analytics** – We can run real-time streaming data analytics by using Amazon Kinesis.

Limits of Amazon Kinesis?

Following are certain limits that should be kept in mind while using Amazon Kinesis Streams —

- Records of a stream can be accessible up to 24 hours by default and can be extended up to 7 days by enabling extended data retention.
- The maximum size of a data blob (the data payload before Base64-encoding) in one record is 1 megabyte (MB).
- One shard supports up to 1000 PUT records per second.
- For more information related to limits, visit the following link — https://docs.aws.amazon.com/kinesis/latest/dev/service-sizes-and-limits.html

How to Use Amazon Kinesis?

Following are the steps to use Amazon Kinesis —

Step 1 — Set up Kinesis Stream using the following steps —

- Sign into AWS account. Select Amazon Kinesis from Amazon Management Console.
- Click the Create stream and fill the required fields such as stream name and number of shards. Click the Create button.

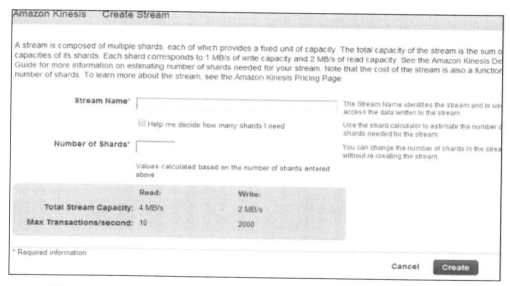

- The Stream will now be visible in the Stream List.

Step 2 — Set up users on Kinesis stream. Create New Users & assign a policy to each user.(We have discussed the procedure above to create Users and assigning policy to them)

Step 3 – Connect your application to Amazon Kinesis; here we are connecting Zoomdata to Amazon Kinesis. Following are the steps to connect.

- Log in to Zoomdata as Administrator and click Sources in menu.

- Select the Kinesis icon and fill the required details. Click the Next button.

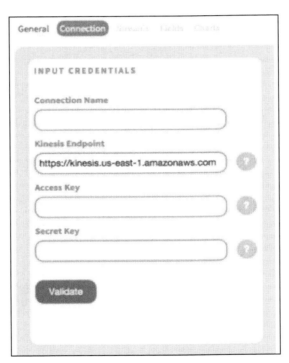

- Select the desired Stream on the Stream tab.
- On the Fields tab, create unique label names, as required and click the Next button.

154

- On the Charts Tab, enable the charts for data. Customize the settings as required and then click the Finish button to save the setting.

Features of Amazon Kinesis

- **Real-time processing** — It allows to collect and analyze information in real-time like stock trade prices otherwise we need to wait for data-out report.
- **Easy to use** — Using Amazon Kinesis, we can create a new stream, set its requirements, and start streaming data quickly.
- **High throughput, elastic** — It allows to collect and analyze information in real-time like stock trade prices otherwise we need to wait for data-out report.
- **Integrate with other Amazon services** — It can be integrated with Amazon Redshift, Amazon S3 and Amazon DynamoDB.
- **Build kinesis applications** — Amazon Kinesis provides the developers with client libraries that enable the design and operation of real-time data processing applications. Add the Amazon Kinesis Client Library to Java application and it will notify when new data is available for processing.
- **Cost-efficient** — Amazon Kinesis is cost-efficient for workloads of any scale. Pay as we go for the resources used and pay hourly for the throughput required.

Amazon Web Services - Elastic MapReduce

Amazon Elastic MapReduce (EMR) is a web service that provides a managed framework to run data processing frameworks such as Apache Hadoop, Apache Spark, and Presto in an easy, cost-effective, and secure manner.

It is used for data analysis, web indexing, data warehousing, financial analysis, scientific simulation, etc.

How to Set Up Amazon EMR?

Follow these steps to set up Amazon EMR —

Step 1 — Sign in to AWS account and select Amazon EMR on management console.

Step 2 — Create Amazon S3 bucket for cluster logs & output data. (Procedure is explained in detail in Amazon S3 section)

Step 3 — Launch Amazon EMR cluster.

Following are the steps to create cluster and launch it to EMR.

- Use this link to open Amazon EMR console — https://console.aws.amazon.com/elasticmapreduce/home
- Select create cluster and provide the required details on Cluster Configuration page.

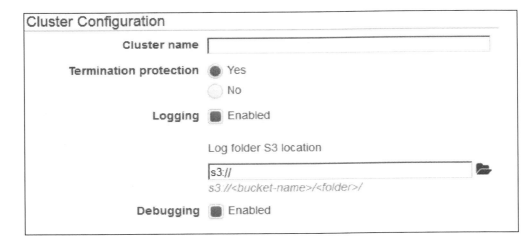

- Leave the Tags section options as default and proceed.
- On the Software configuration section, level the options as default.

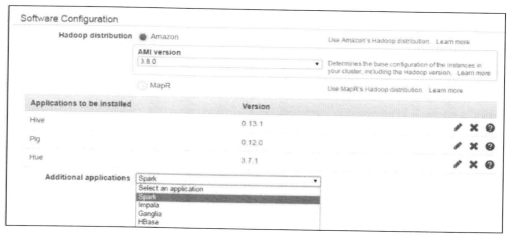

- On the File System Configuration section, leave the options for EMRFS as set by default. EMRFS is an implementation of HDFS, it allows Amazon EMR clusters to store data on Amazon S3.

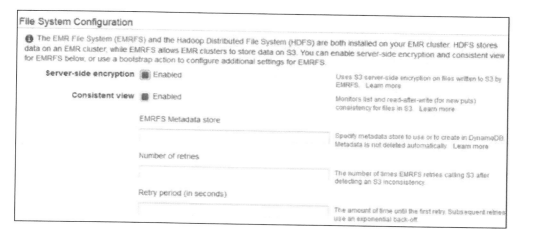

- On the Hardware Configuration section, select m3.xlarge in EC2 instance type field and leave other settings as default. Click the Next button.

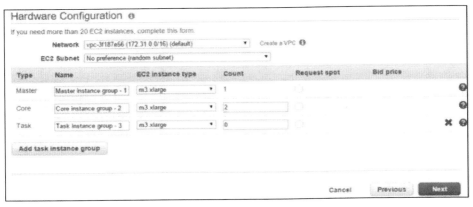

- On the Security and Access section, for EC2 key pair, select the pair from the list in EC2 key pair field and leave the other settings as default.
- On Bootstrap Actions section, leave the fields as set by default and click the Add button. Bootstrap actions are scripts that are executed during the setup before Hadoop starts on every cluster node.
- On the Steps section, leave the settings as default and proceed.
- Click the Create Cluster button and the Cluster Details page opens. This is where we should run the Hive script as a cluster step and use the Hue web interface to query the data.

Step 4 – Run the Hive script using the following steps.

• Open the Amazon EMR console and select the desired cluster.
• Move to the Steps section and expand it. Then click the Add step button.
• The Add Step dialog box opens. Fill the required fields, then click the Add button.

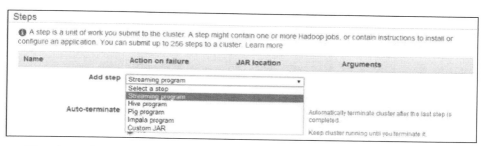

• To view the output of Hive script, use the following steps –
○ Open the Amazon S3 console and select S3 bucket used for the output data.
○ Select the output folder.
○ The query writes the results into a separate folder. Select **os_requests**.
○ The output is stored in a text file. This file can be downloaded.

161

Benefits of Amazon EMR

Following are the benefits of Amazon EMR –

- **Easy to use** – Amazon EMR is easy to use, i.e. it is easy to set up cluster, Hadoop configuration, node provisioning, etc.
- **Reliable** – It is reliable in the sense that it retries failed tasks and automatically replaces poorly performing instances.
- **Elastic** – Amazon EMR allows to compute large amount of instances to process data at any scale. It easily increases or decreases the number of instances.
- **Secure** – It automatically configures Amazon EC2 firewall settings, controls network access to instances, launch clusters in an Amazon VPC, etc.
- **Flexible** – It allows complete control over the clusters and root access to every instance. It also allows installation of additional applications and customizes your cluster as per requirement.
- **Cost-efficient** – Its pricing is easy to estimate. It charges hourly for every instance used.

Amazon Web Services - Data Pipeline

AWS Data Pipeline is a web service, designed to make it easier for users to integrate data spread across multiple AWS services and analyze it from a single location.

Using AWS Data Pipeline, data can be accessed from the source, processed, and then the results can be efficiently transferred to the respective AWS services.

How to Set Up Data Pipeline?

Following are the steps to set up data pipeline −

Step 1 − Create the Pipeline using the following steps.

- Sign-in to AWS account.
- Use this link to Open AWS Data Pipeline console − https://console.aws.amazon.com/datapipeline/
- Select the region in the navigation bar.
- Click the Create New Pipeline button.
- Fill the required details in the respective fields.
    - In the Source field, choose Build using a template and then select this template − Getting Started using ShellCommandActivity.

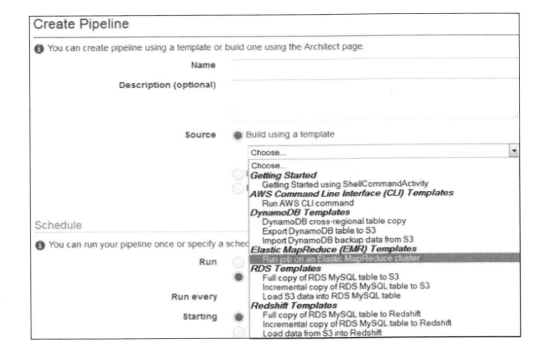

- The Parameters section opens only when the template is selected. Leave the S3 input folder and Shell command to run with their default values. Click the folder icon next to S3 output folder, and select the buckets.
- In Schedule, leave the values as default.
- In Pipeline Configuration, leave the logging as enabled. Click the folder icon under S3 location for logs and select the buckets.
- In Security/Access, leave IAM roles values as default.
- Click the Activate button.

How to Delete a Pipeline?

Deleting the pipeline will also delete all associated objects.

Step 1 — Select the pipeline from the pipelines list.

Step 2 — Click the Actions button and then choose Delete.

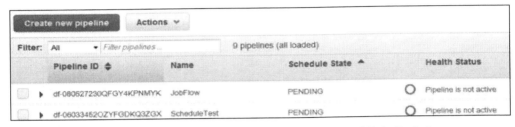

Step 3 — A confirmation prompt window opens. Click Delete.

Features of AWS Data Pipeline

Simple and cost-efficient – Its drag-and-drop features makes it easy to create a pipeline on console. Its visual pipeline creator provides a library of pipeline templates. These templates make it easier to create pipelines for tasks like processing log files, archiving data to Amazon S3, etc.

Reliable – Its infrastructure is designed for fault tolerant execution activities. If failures occur in the activity logic or data sources, then AWS Data Pipeline automatically retries the activity. If the failure continues, then it will send a failure notification. We can even configure these notification alerts for situations like successful runs, failure, delays in activities, etc.

Flexible – AWS Data Pipeline provides various features like scheduling, tracking, error handling, etc. It can be configured to take actions like run Amazon EMR jobs, execute SQL queries directly against databases, execute custom applications running on Amazon EC2, etc.

Amazon Web Services - Machine Learning

Amazon Machine Learning is a service that allows to develop predictive applications by using algorithms, mathematical models based on the user's data.

Amazon Machine Learning reads data through Amazon S3, Redshift and RDS, then visualizes the data through the AWS Management Console and the Amazon Machine Learning API. This data can be imported or exported to other AWS services via S3 buckets.

It uses "industry-standard logistic regression" algorithm to generate models.

Types of Tasks Performed by Amazon Machine Learning

Three different types of tasks can be performed by Amazon Machine learning service —

• A binary classification model can predict one of the two possible results, i.e. either yes or no.
• A multi-class classification model can predict multiple conditions. For example, it can track a customer's online orders.
• A regression model results in an exact value. Regression models can predict the best-selling price for a product or the number of units that will sell.

How to Use Amazon Machine Learning?

Step 1 – Sign in to AWS account and select Machine Learning. Click the Get Started button.

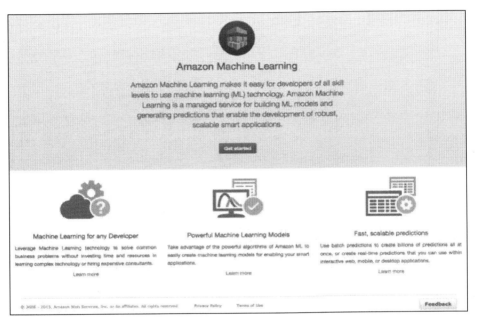

Step 2 – Select Standard Setup and then click Launch.

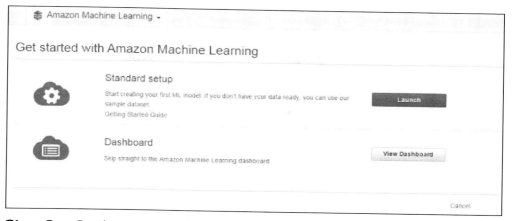

Step 3 – In the Input data section, fill the required details and select the choice for data storage, either S3 or Redshift. Click the Verify button.

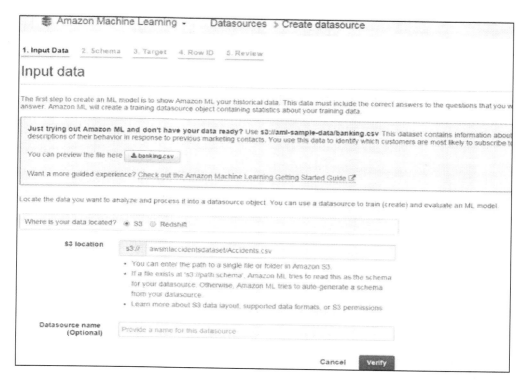

Step 4 – After S3 location verification is completed, Schema section opens. Fill the fields as per requirement and proceed to the next step.

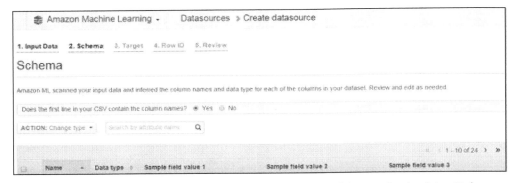

Step 5 – In Target section, reselect the variables selected in Schema section and proceed to the next step.

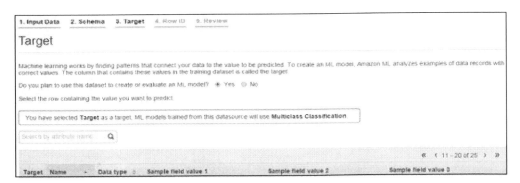

Step 6 – Leave the values as default in Row ID section and proceed to the Review section. Verify the details and click the Continue button.

Following are some screenshots of Machine Learning services.

Data Set Created by Machine Learning

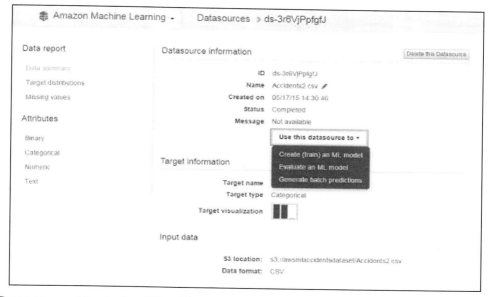

Summary Made by Machine Learning

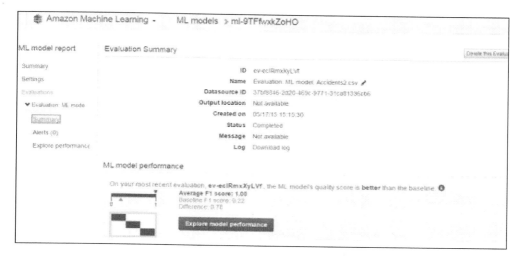

Exploring Performance Using Machine Learning

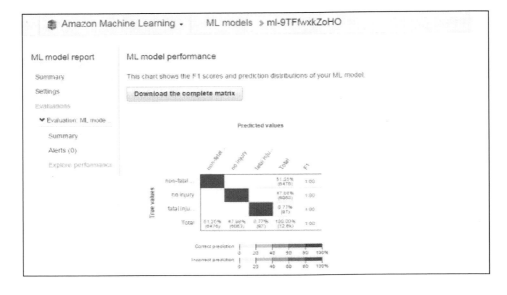

Features of Amazon Machine Learning

Easy to create machine learning models – It is easy to create ML models from data stored in Amazon S3, Amazon Redshift, Amazon RDS and query these models for predictions by using Amazon ML APIs and wizards.

High performance – Amazon ML prediction APIs can be used further to generate billions of predictions for the applications. We can use them within interactive web, mobile, or desktop applications.

Cost-efficient – Pay only for what we use without any setup charges and no upfront commitments.

AWS - Simple WorkFlow Service

The following services fall under Application Services section —

- Amazon CloudSearch
- Amazon Simple Queue Services (SQS)
- Amazon Simple Notification Services (SNS)
- Amazon Simple Email Services (SES)
- Amazon SWF

In this chapter, we will discuss Amazon SWF.

Amazon Simple Workflow Service (SWF) is a task based API that makes it easy to coordinate work across distributed application components. It provides a programming model and infrastructure for coordinating distributed components and maintaining their execution state in a reliable way. Using Amazon SWF, we can focus on building the aspects of the application that differentiates it.

A **workflow** is a set of activities that carry out some objective, including logic that coordinates the activities to achieve the desired output.

Workflow history consists of complete and consistent record of each event that occurred since the workflow execution started. It is maintained by SWF.

How to Use SWF?

Step 1 – Sign in to AWS account and select SWF on the Services dashboard.

Step 2 – Click the Launch Sample Walkthrough button.

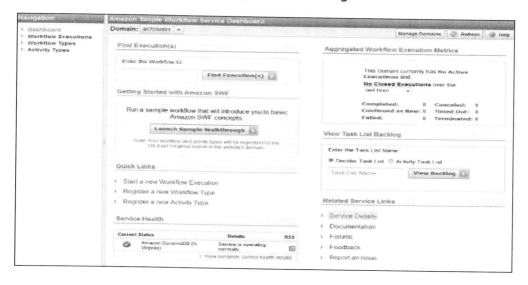

Step 3 – Run a Sample Workflow window opens. Click the Get Started button.

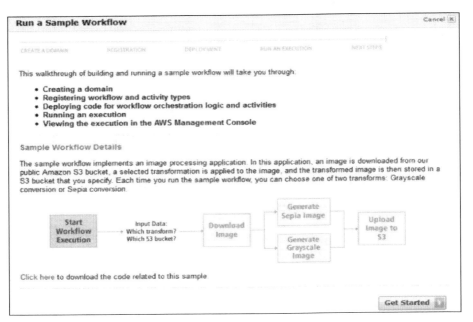

Step 4 – In the Create Domain section, click the Create a new Domain radio button and then click the Continue button.

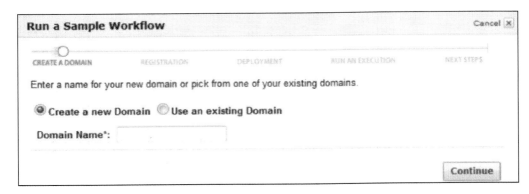

Step 5 – In Registration section, read the instructions then click the Continue button.

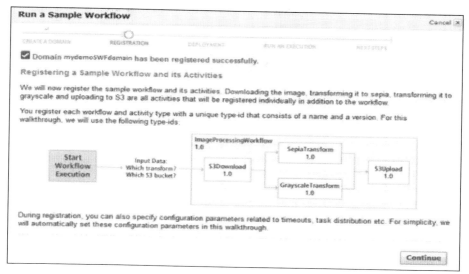

Step 6 – In the Deployment section, choose the desired option and click the Continue button.

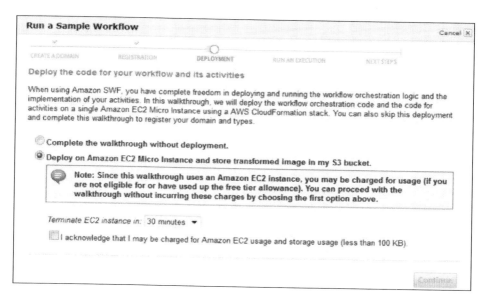

Step 7 – In the Run an Execution section, choose the desired option and click the Run this Execution button.

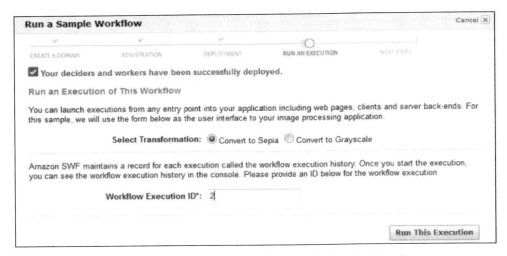

Finally, SWF will be created and will be available in the list.

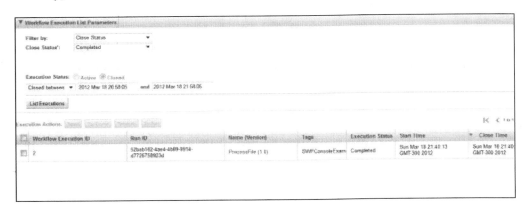

Benefits of Amazon SWF

- It enables applications to be stateless, because all information about a workflow execution is stored in its workflow history.
- For each workflow execution, the history provides a record of which activities were scheduled, their current statuses and results. The workflow execution uses this information to determine the next steps.
- The history provides steps in detail that can be used to monitor running workflow executions and verify completed workflow executions.

Amazon Web Services - WorkMail

Amazon WorkMail was formerly known as Zocalo. It is a managed email and calendaring service that runs in Cloud. It provides security controls and is designed to work with your existing PC and Mac-based Outlook clients including the prepackaged Click-to-Run versions. It also works with mobile clients that speak the Exchange ActiveSync protocol.

Its migration tool allows to move mailboxes from on-premises email servers to the service, and works with any device that supports the Microsoft Exchange ActiveSync protocol, such as Apple's iPad and iPhone, Google Android, and Windows Phone.

How to Use Amazon WorkMail?

Step 1 – Sign in to AWS account and open the Amazon WorkMail console using the following link – https://console.aws.amazon.com/workmail/

Step 2 – Click the Get Started button.

Step 3 – Select the desired option and choose the Region from the top right side of the navigation bar.

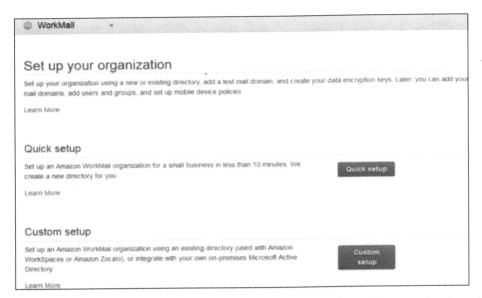

Step 4 — Fill the required details and proceed to the next step to configure an account. Follow the instructions. Finally, the mailbox will look like as shown in the following screenshot.

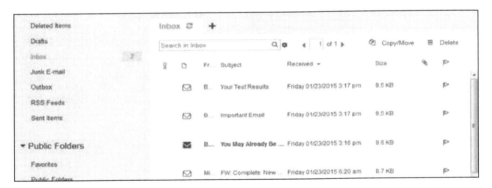

Features of Amazon WorkMail

Secure – Amazon WorkMail automatically encrypts entire data with the encryption keys using the AWS Key Management Service.

Managed – Amazon WorkMail offers complete control over email and there is no need to worry about installing a software, maintaining and managing hardware. Amazon WorkMail automatically handles all these needs.

Accessibility – Amazon WorkMail supports Microsoft Outlook on both Windows and Mac OS X. Hence, users can use the existing email client without any additional requirements.

Availability – Users can synchronize emails, contacts and calendars with iOS, Android, Windows Phone, etc. using the Microsoft Exchange ActiveSync protocol anywhere.

Cost-efficient – Amazon WorkMail charges 4$ per user per month up to 50GB of storage.

Made in the USA
Lexington, KY
14 May 2018